I0020743

Instant Silverlight 5 Animation

Enrich your web page or Silverlight business application
with Silverlight animations

Nick Polyak

PUBLISHING

BIRMINGHAM - MUMBAI

Instant Silverlight 5 Animation

Copyright © 2013 Packt Publishing

All rights reserved. No part of this book may be reproduced, stored in a retrieval system, or transmitted in any form or by any means, without the prior written permission of the publisher, except in the case of brief quotations embedded in critical articles or reviews.

Every effort has been made in the preparation of this book to ensure the accuracy of the information presented. However, the information contained in this book is sold without warranty, either express or implied. Neither the author, nor Packt Publishing, and its dealers and distributors will be held liable for any damages caused or alleged to be caused directly or indirectly by this book.

Packt Publishing has endeavored to provide trademark information about all of the companies and products mentioned in this book by the appropriate use of capitals. However, Packt Publishing cannot guarantee the accuracy of this information.

First published: January 2013

Production Reference: 1160113

Published by Packt Publishing Ltd.
Livery Place
35 Livery Street
Birmingham B3 2PB, UK.

ISBN 978-1-84968-714-0

www.packtpub.com

Credits

Author
Nick Polyak

Reviewer
Thomas Martinsen

Acquisition Editor
Rukhsana Khambatta

Commissioning Editor
Meeta Rajani

Technical Editor
Jalasha D'costa

Project Coordinator
Shraddha Bagadia
Esha Thakker

Proofreader
Bernadette Watkins

Indexer
Rekha Nair

Graphics
Sheetal Aute

Production Coordinator
Melwyn D'sa

Cover Work
Melwyn D'sa

Cover Image
Sheetal Aute

About the Author

Nick Polyak is a technology enthusiast who enjoys building software and learning new technologies. For the past six years, Nick worked primarily on Silverlight/WPF projects, and prior to that he worked with C++ and Java. Nick is looking forward to harnessing the new capabilities coming with HTML5 and modern JavaScript libraries.

Nick got his Ph.D. from Rensselaer Polytechnic Institute in 1998. He did his research in Wavelet based image processing and published a number of papers on the subject.

More recently Nick published several articles on codeproject.com some of which (a Prism tutorial and an article on MVVM) became quite popular.

Nick is the owner of the AWebPros.com consulting company.

I would like to thank my wife and children for being patient with me while I worked on this book.

About the Reviewer

Thomas Martinsen is a passionate developer with a focus on Windows development. Thomas is a regular speaker at customer-oriented and developer-oriented events, having worked as a consultant for more than 10 years.

Thomas is a partner in Bluefragments, a company with a focus on the newest Microsoft technologies. Bluefragments is among the best Windows developers in Denmark and has recently built a series of Windows 8 apps for the Windows Store.

For three years now, Thomas been awarded Microsoft MVP.

www.PacktPub.com

Support files, eBooks, discount offers and more

You might want to visit www.PacktPub.com for support files and downloads related to your book.

Did you know that Packt offers eBook versions of every book published, with PDF and ePub files available? You can upgrade to the eBook version at www.PacktPub.com and as a print book customer, you are entitled to a discount on the eBook copy. Get in touch with us at service@packtpub.com for more details.

At www.PacktPub.com, you can also read a collection of free technical articles, sign up for a range of free newsletters and receive exclusive discounts and offers on Packt books and eBooks.

http://PacktLib.PacktPub.com

Do you need instant solutions to your IT questions? PacktLib is Packt's online digital book library. Here, you can access, read and search across Packt's entire library of books.

Why Subscribe?

- Fully searchable across every book published by Packt
- Copy and paste, print and bookmark content
- On demand and accessible via web browser

Free Access for Packt account holders

If you have an account with Packt at www.PacktPub.com, you can use this to access PacktLib today and view nine entirely free books. Simply use your login credentials for immediate access.

Instant Updates on New Packt Books

Get notified! Find out when new books are published by following @PacktEnterprise on Twitter, or the *Packt Enterprise* Facebook page.

Table of Contents

Preface

What is Silverlight

Silverlight is a relatively new technology introduced by Microsoft in order to enable the developers to build multi-platform client GUI applications that can run within or outside of Internet browsers.

Why should I use Silverlight

Silverlight empowers developers with great new GUI capabilities, combined with revolutionary GUI coding concepts that came to Silverlight from WPF. While some think that HTML 5 gives the developers functionality that is almost as powerful as Silverlight, the programming model of HTML 5 is indisputably old, while the Silverlight/WPF programming model is ahead of that of any competing software.

Unlike the currently available versions of HTML, Silverlight is 98 percent multi-platform (between Windows and Macs) and its list of non multi-platform features is freely available. As long as you avoid using those features, any application you build for Windows is guaranteed to run on Mac.

Silverlight is close to being 100 percent multi-browser (if there are any features that do not perform the same on different browsers, I am not aware of them) and any application you write using Internet Explorer is guaranteed to run within Firefox on the same platform, while this might not be the case with HTML.

Silverlight has a very small footprint – in order to make Silverlight 5 run on your machine you need to download and install only a 6 MB package.

Silverlight makes it very easy to deploy your application via the Internet, whether it is a browser-based application or not.

Microsoft Phone uses Silverlight as its primary coding platform.

What is the downside of using Silverlight

Microsoft pedalled back on Silverlight as they decided that Silverlight might undermine their Windows platform. The Windows 8 platform uses many Silverlight concepts, but is strictly Windows oriented.

Apple does not allow plugins for their iPhone and iPad browsers, since plugins undermine their Apple store application model. Microsoft followed suit and Windows 8 browsers for tablets and phones will not support Silverlight as a browser plugin. To the best of my knowledge, Windows 8 tablets will continue to run Silverlight applications outside of browsers. The Windows 8 programing model, however, is very similar to Silverlight and it should be easy to convert your Silverlight application to Windows 8.

There is a lot of buzz around HTML 5 being able to do everything that Silverlight does, and, undeniably, the HTML 5 application will run on the platforms so far closed to Silverlight – iPads, iPhones, and Android systems. From my point of view, while HTML 5 is a great technology, it does not address the questions that have plagued the HTML/JavaScript technology from the outset – namely its programming paradigms are not strong enough to support coding complex business logic. Additionally, HTML 5 will not run on many of the existing desktop browsers, so if someone wants to build a website available to everyone they usually have to use HTML 4.

What this book covers

This book is about creating animations using Silverlight technology.

Chapter 1, Building Blocks of Animation, talks about the Silverlight concepts used for animation: dependency and attached properties, bindings, transforms, and storyboards.

Chapter 2, Animations in Business Logic Silverlight Applications, talks about using `VisualStateManager` for custom control animations and animation navigation transitions.

Chapter 3, Creating Animated Textures, talks about using Perlin noise for generating random processes such as clouds and fire.

Chapter 4, 3D Animations in Silverlight, talks about using Perspective Transform for simple 3D animations and also covers using a subset of the XNA functionality in Silverlight for more complex animations.

Chapter 5, Building an Animated Banner, talks about creating a Silverlight animated banner and integrating it into an HTML page.

What you need for this book

The following software should be installed in order for the reader to be able to run the samples:

1. MS Visual Studio 2010 Professional (a trial version can be downloaded from `http://www.microsoft.com/en-us/download/details.aspx?id=2890` and will run for a period of time without requiring the user to purchase a license).

2. MS Visual Studio 2010 SP1 can be downloaded free from `http://www.microsoft.com/en-us/download/details.aspx?id=23691`. It should only be installed after the installation of Visual Studio.

3. Silverlight 5 tools for Visual Studio 2010 SP1 can be downloaded free from `http://www.microsoft.com/en-us/download/details.aspx?id=28358`.

Who this book is for

We assume that the reader already has basic knowledge of Silverlight or WPF programming concepts. One should not use this book to learn Silverlight or WPF basics.

Notes on the samples

We recommend that you create and build all the samples from scratch, using the source code provided with the book just as a way to check your work.

WPF experts with no previous Silverlight experience might have difficulty creating, starting, and understanding Silverlight applications, so there is *Appendix A, Creating and starting a Silverlight project*, describing how to do it.

Silverlight only has a subset of WPF functionality, for example, it does not have data and property triggers, and its event triggers can only react to a loaded event. MS Expression Blend SDK provides functionality to mitigate these deficiencies, as well as many other exciting features. Expression Blend SDK DLLs are free and fully redistributable and are provided with the samples under the `MSExpressionBlendSDKDll` folder. Expression Blend SDK does not require Expression Blend (which we are not using anyways).

Follow the instructions within *Appendix B, Changing the XAML formatting*, if you want to format your XAML file to have each XML attribute on a separate line as we do in our sample code.

In order to format your C# code similar to the code in our samples, please install and use the snippets provided under the `Snippets` folder (which is part of the sample code that comes with the book). Information on installing and using snippets is available in *Appendix C, Installing snippets*, and *Appendix D, Using snippets*, respectively.

Conventions

In this book, you will find a number of styles of text that distinguish between different kinds of information. Here are some examples of these styles, and an explanation of their meaning.

Code words in text are shown as follows: "We can include other contexts through the use of the `include` directive."

A block of code is set as follows:

```
public double RotationAngle
{
    get { return (double)GetValue(RotationAngleProperty); }
    set { SetValue(RotationAngleProperty, value); }
}
```

New terms and important words are shown in bold. Words that you see on the screen, in menus or dialog boxes, for example, appear in the text like this: "You can start the browser displaying our Silverlight banner within that HTML page by right-clicking on the file within **Solution Explorer** and choosing **View in Browser**".

 Warnings or important notes appear in a box like this.

Tips and tricks appear like this.

Reader feedback

Feedback from our readers is always welcome. Let us know what you think about this book—what you liked or may have disliked. Reader feedback is important for us to develop titles that you really get the most out of.

To send us general feedback, simply send an e-mail to feedback@packtpub.com, and mention the book title through the subject of your message.

If there is a topic that you have expertise in and you are interested in either writing or contributing to a book, see our author guide on www.packtpub.com/authors.

Customer support

Now that you are the proud owner of a Packt book, we have a number of things to help you to get the most from your purchase.

Downloading the example code

You can download the example code files for all Packt books you have purchased from your account at http://www.packtpub.com. If you purchased this book elsewhere, you can visit http://www.packtpub.com/support and register to have the files e-mailed directly to you.

Errata

Although we have taken every care to ensure the accuracy of our content, mistakes do happen. If you find a mistake in one of our books—maybe a mistake in the text or the code—we would be grateful if you would report this to us. By doing so, you can save other readers from frustration and help us improve subsequent versions of this book. If you find any errata, please report them by visiting http://www.packtpub.com/support, selecting your book, clicking on the errata submission form link, and entering the details of your errata. Once your errata are verified, your submission will be accepted and the errata will be uploaded to our website, or added to any list of existing errata, under the Errata section of that title.

Piracy

Piracy of copyright material on the Internet is an ongoing problem across all media. At Packt, we take the protection of our copyright and licenses very seriously. If you come across any illegal copies of our works, in any form, on the Internet, please provide us with the location address or website name immediately so that we can pursue a remedy.

Please contact us at `copyright@packtpub.com` with a link to the suspected pirated material.

We appreciate your help in protecting our authors, and our ability to bring you valuable content.

Questions

You can contact us at `questions@packtpub.com` if you are having a problem with any aspect of the book, and we will do our best to address it.

Building Blocks of Animation

This chapter describes Silverlight/WPF concepts needed for creating animations, namely dependency and attached properties, bindings, transforms, and storyboards. We assume that the reader is already familiar with most of the concepts within this section and uses it simply as a refresher, as well as a way to jump-start the samples for the rest of the application.

In this chapter we will look at:

- **Dependency properties**: These are a special type of properties that can be animated using the storyboards in Silverlight.

- **Attached properties**: These are very similar to dependency properties except that they do not have to be defined in a class that uses them.

- **Bindings**: These bind two properties together so that when one changes the other does as well.

- **Transforms**: These are used to modify the visual elements. Transforms are often used for animations.

- **Storyboards**: These are objects that encapsulate information about animations including what properties are animated and how.

Spinning control sample

We will start developing a simple control sample and gradually expand it to demonstrate all the required concepts.

The resulting sample application is located under `CODE\SpinningControlSample\SpinningControlSample.sln`, but we recommend that you build this sample from scratch, based on the instructions within this chapter.

The goal of this sample is to develop a **lookless** control that has a `RotationAngle` dependency property and later to provide a view for this control (for example, as a rectangle), and to animate the `RotationAngle` so that the rectangle would be seen as rotating.

Lookless controls are controls that do not contain any visual implementation details. Such controls need a `ControlTemplate` in order to display them. This provides a great advantage to developers/designers because it separates the control's implementation details from its presentation.

Firstly, let's create a **Silverlight Application** project called `SpinningControlSample`. Follow the instructions in *Appendix A, Creating and Starting a Silverlight Project*, to create a browser-based, empty Silverlight solution. As mentioned in *Appendix A*, the solution will actually contain two projects, `SpinningControlSample` and `SpinningControlSample.Web`. The project with the `.Web` extension is just an ASP project to embed the Silverlight page. We are not going to concentrate on it. The real project of interest to us is `SpinningControlSample`.

Within the `SpinningControlSample` project, we create a new empty C# class, `SpinningControl`.

Make the `SpinningControl` class inherit from the `Control` class as shown in the following code snippet:

```
public class SpinningControl : Control
{

}
```

We are going to populate this class to provide the functionality that is previously described.

Defining a dependency property in C# code

Dependency properties (DPs) are a special type of properties introduced in WPF and Silverlight. Just like the usual .NET properties, they describe a property of a .NET object. Unlike the usual .NET properties, their storage does not take space within the class that uses them. Rather, they are stored in some static collections, indexed, and accessed by the corresponding objects.

Silverlight and WPF provide natural ways to animate the dependency properties using Storyboard objects (which are described later in the chapter).

Silverlight and WPF also have natural mechanisms to bind two dependency properties together (or a usual property to a dependency property) so that changing one of them will trigger the other to change.

Now let's define the `RotationAngle` dependency property of a type `double` within this class. Put the cursor between the curly brackets defining the body of the class and type `propdp` followed by a tab `keystroke`. Follow the instructions in *Appendix D, Using Snippets*, to set up the name, type, and default value of the property.

```
public class SpinningControl : Control
{
    #region RotationAngle Dependency Property
    // Dependency Properties' getter and setter for accessing the
    //DP as
    // if it is a usual property
    public double RotationAngle
    {
        get { return (double)GetValue(RotationAngleProperty); }
        set { SetValue(RotationAngleProperty, value); }
    }

    // static field for storing and accessing the DPs by object
        //reference
    public static readonly DependencyProperty
RotationAngleProperty = DependencyProperty.Register
    (
        "RotationAngle",                    // DP name
        typeof(double),                     // DP type
        typeof(SpinningControl),            // Class defining the DP
        new PropertyMetadata(0.0)           // DP's default value
    );
    #endregion RotationAngle Dependency Property
}
```

You might have noticed that the `RotationAngle` property within the `SpinningControl` class does not refer to any object field. Rather, it uses `GetValue` and `SetValue` methods inherited from `DependencyObject` to get and set the dependency objects correspondingly. The field values themselves are stored within the `RotationAngleProperty` static class member, and individual objects of the class `SpinningControl` get their `RotationAngle` property values from this static field via their object reference (using the functionality embedded within the `DependencyObject` class).

This is one of the advantages of using the dependency properties – the SpinningControl object that does not set the property does not need any extra space for this property; it gets the default from the static RotationAngleProperty structure defined once for all the objects of the same class. Take a look at the following section within DP's definition:

```
public double RotationAngle
{
    get { return (double)GetValue(RotationAngleProperty); }
    set { SetValue(RotationAngleProperty, value); }
}
```

It provides a way to access the dependency property as a usual .NET property. Many .NET calls to the DP, however, are not using these get and set accessors; instead such calls use the DependencyObject class GetValue() and SetValue() methods directly. Because of this, you should not add any code to these property accessors – such a code simply won't be executed in many cases.

This is all we need to define a lookless control – just a class extending Control and containing some non-visual properties (usually DPs), functions, and events. Such a control is called *lookless* because it does not define any visual presentation for itself. Visual presentation of a lookless control is defined by a control template, which is usually represented by XAML code residing in some XAML resource file. The advantage of lookless controls lies in the fact that you do not have to change the control itself in order to achieve various different visual representations. All you need to do is to change the template. Since it is the control itself and not its template that is responsible for interacting with the rest of the application, by changing the templates one can completely change the visual presentation of the application without affecting any underlying logic. More on lookless controls can be found at http://tinyurl.com/lookless.

For most of the samples within this book, I am using lookless controls since this is the best practice, even though it is not related to the subject of animations.

Defining visual presentation for spinning control

Now we are going to add code to MainPage.xaml to display a SpinningControl object. When you open the MainPage.xaml file, you will see the following XAML code created for you by Visual Studio:

```
<UserControl
    x:Class="SpinningControlSample.MainPage"
    xmlns="http://schemas.microsoft.com/winfx/2006/xaml/presentation"
    xmlns:x="http://schemas.microsoft.com/winfx/2006/xaml"
    xmlns:d="http://schemas.microsoft.com/expression/blend/2008"
    xmlns:mc="http://schemas.openxmlformats.org/markup-
compatibility/2006"
    xmlns:i="http://schemas.microsoft.com/expression/2010/
interactivity"
    xmlns:se="http://schemas.microsoft.com/expression/2010/
interactions"
    xmlns:SpinningControlSample="clr-namespace:SpinningControlSample"
    mc:Ignorable="d"
    d:DesignHeight="300"
    d:DesignWidth="400">
    <Grid x:Name="LayoutRoot" Background="White">

    </Grid>
</UserControl>
```

Let's modify this class to display our SpinningControl object as a rectangle rotated by an angle specified by its RotationAngle property:

```
<UserControl x:Class="SpinningControlSample.MainPage"
                . . .
                d:DesignHeight="300"
                d:DesignWidth="400">
    <Grid x:Name="LayoutRoot" Background="White">
        <!--Dependency Property RotationAngle is referred to within
        XAML in exactly the same way as the usual
         property (as in the line below)-->
        <SpinningControlSample:SpinningControl
x:Name="TheSpinningControl"
                                        RotationAngle="45">
            <SpinningControlSample:SpinningControl.Template>
                <!-- SpinningControl's template is set to create a
visual
                    representation for the control. -->
            <ControlTemplate
                TargetType="SpinningControlSample:SpinningControl">
                <Rectangle Fill="Orange"
                            Width="100"
                            Height="30"
                            RenderTransformOrigin="0.5,0.5">
                    <Rectangle.RenderTransform>
```

```
                                 <!-- We use "Binding" to connect
                                      RotateTransform's Angle property
                                      to the RotationAngle Dependency
                                      Property. -->
                                 <RotateTransform
                                     Angle="{Binding
                                             Path=RotationAngle,
                                             Mode=OneWay,
                                             RelativeSource=
                                             {RelativeSource
                                                Mode=TemplatedParent}}"
     />
                             </Rectangle.RenderTransform>
                         </Rectangle>
                     </ControlTemplate>
                 </SpinningControlSample:SpinningControl.Template>
             </SpinningControlSample:SpinningControl>
         </Grid>
     </UserControl>
```

If you build and run the SpinningControlSample solution, you will get a 45 degree rotated orange rectangle displayed in a browser window as shown in the following screenshot:

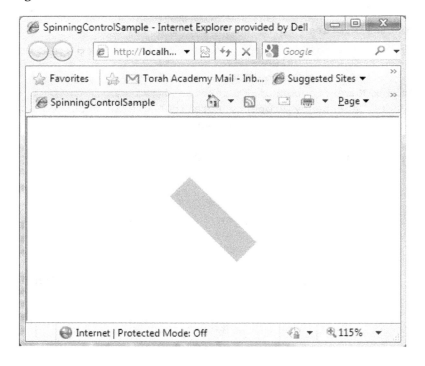

Note that we defined the template for our lookless control inline
(see the `<SpinningControlSample:SpinningControl.Template>` tag).

Bindings

Binding is a powerful Silverlight/WPF concept allowing two or more properties on
two objects to be tied together, so that when one of them changes, the other changes
as well. One of the binding's properties is called **source property** and the other **target
property**. Usually we assume that the target property changes when the source
does, but if the binding mode is *two-way*, the opposite is also true, that is, a change
in the source property will be triggered by a change in the target property. The
target property should always be a dependency property while the source property
can be a usual .NET one. More on bindings can be found at http://tinyurl.com/
wpfbindings.

The XAML code presented in the previous subsection uses binding to bind the
`RotationAngle` dependency property of the `SpinningControl` object to the `Angle`
property of the `RotateTransform` object:

```
<RotateTransform Angle="{Binding Path=RotationAngle,
                        Mode=OneWay,
                        RelativeSource={RelativeSource

Mode=TemplatedParent}}" />
```

In this case, the `RotationAngle` property of the `SpinningControl` object is the
source property of the **binding**, while the `Angle` property of the `RotateTransform`
object is its target property. The binding mode being set to `OneWay` specifies that the
target property changes whenever the source property does, but not vice versa. The
`RelativeSource` property of the binding, when set to `TemplatedParent`, specifies
that the binding's source property is chosen by the `Path` property taken with respect
to the control to which the template applies (in our case it is `SpinningControl`).

Transforms

Silverlight provides a powerful set of transforms to apply to the visual object.
The following is a full set of 2D transforms:

- `TranslateTransform`: This shifts an object in a 2D plane.

- `ScaleTransform`: This scales (or resizes) the object by the `ScaleX` factor
  along the X-axis and the `ScaleY` factor along the Y-axis.

- `SkewTransform`: Skewing along the *X*-axis turns every vector orthogonal to the *X*-axis by the same angle defined by `AngleX`, and expands its length so that its *Y* coordinate stays the same. The `AngleY` parameter of the transform is in charge of skewing along the *Y*-axis.
- `RotateTransform`: This rotates an object by the `Angle` parameter.
- `MatrixTransform`: This is a generic transform that can represent any linear transformation and translation within a 2D plane.

We previously used `RotateTransform` to rotate the rectangle.

There is also the `PlaneProjection` transform imitating the moving of an object in a 3D space. We will describe this transform in detail later in the book.

Storyboards and animations

Storyboards are Silverlight entities that are used for describing the animations of various dependency and attached properties. They consist of one or several animation entities each one of which is dedicated to animating just one dependency property. This section gives an overview of storyboard and animation functionality.

Adding a rotation animation to our code

We are about to make this rectangle rotate by changing the dependency property, that is, `RotationAngle` using a **storyboard**.

The storyboard can be created as the page's resource by adding the following XAML code above the `<Grid  x:Name="LayoutRoot" ...>` line:

```
<Storyboard
    x:Key="RotationStoryboard"
      Storyboard.TargetName="TheSpinningControl"
      Storyboard.TargetProperty="(SpinningControlSample:
                                  SpinningControl.RotationAngle)">
    <DoubleAnimation BeginTime="00:00:00"
                     Duration="00:00:01"
                     From="0"
                     To="360"
                     RepeatBehavior="Forever" />
</Storyboard>
```

Once this storyboard runs, it will change the `RotationAngle` property on the visual element called `TheSpinningControl` from 0 to 360 over a period of 1 second and then continue repeating the same change forever, which will result in a rotating rectangle.

The only thing remaining is to start the storyboard based on some event.

We are going to add a button at the bottom of the window, which when clicked will start the rotation. Here is the code we need to add to our XAML file under the `</SpinningControl>` end tag in order to create the button:

```
<Button x:Name="StartRotationButton"
        Content="Start Rotation"
        VerticalAlignment="Bottom"
        HorizontalAlignment="Center"
        Margin="0,0,0,20"
        Width="100"
        Height="25">
</Button>
```

It would be easy to get the reference to the button, within the `MainPage.xaml.cs` (code-behind) file and add a handler to the button's `Click` event to pull the storyboard out of the page's resource and start it. However, we do not want to split the button click action triggering a storyboard from the XAML code which defines both the button and the storyboard. This is where MS Expression Blend SDK, mentioned in the *Preface*, comes in handy.

MS Expression Blend SDK does not require having MS Expression Blend installed. It is simply a number of free and redistributable DLLs that make Silverlight/WPF programming easier.

One can download MS Expression Blend SDK using the URL specified in the *Preface*, or simply use the two files, `Microsoft.Expression.Interactions.dll` and `System.Windows.Interactivity.dll`, that come with our code. These files are located in the `MSExpressionBlendSDKDlls` folder and you need to add references to them in our `SpinningControlSample` project. MS Expression Blend SDK allows us to connect the `Click` button event to the `ControlStoryboardAction` functionality that starts the animation without any C# code. Also, we can disable the button once it is clicked, by using MS Expression Blend SDK's `ChangePropertyAction` object.

Add the following namespace reference to the `<UserControl...` tag at the top of the `MainPage.xaml` file:

```
<UserControl …
        …xmlns:i="http://schemas.microsoft.com/expression/2010/
interactivity"
        xmlns:se="http://schemas.microsoft.com/expression/2010/
interactions"
            …/>
```

Now we can use `i:` and `se:` prefixes to access the MS Expression Blend functionality within XAML.

To start the storyboard on a button click, add the following XAML code between the button's start and end tags:

```
<i:Interaction.Triggers>
    <!-- MS Expression Blend SDK trigger will start on "Click"
        event of the button-->
    <i:EventTrigger EventName="Click">
        <!-- ChangePropertyAction below will disable the
StartRotationButton after it is clicked first time -->
        <se:ChangePropertyAction
            TargetObject="{Binding ElementName=StartRotationButton}"
            PropertyName="IsEnabled"
            Value="False" />

        <!-- ControlStoryboardAction will start the RotationStoryboard
-->
        <se:ControlStoryboardAction
            ControlStoryboardOption="Play"
            Storyboard="{StaticResource
RotationStoryboard}" />
    </i:EventTrigger>
</i:Interaction.Triggers>
```

You can run the sample now. Once you click the button, the orange rectangle in the middle starts rotating and the button gets disabled:

A brief overview of different Silverlight animation classes

As we learned earlier, Silverlight Storyboards consist of one or more animation objects. Each animation object controls an animation of one and only one dependency property. Note that only dependency or attached properties can be animated by Silverlight animations. There are two types of animation classes:

- **Simple animations** (that have properties to, from, and by): Such animations change the dependency property linearly in time (unless easing is used). The properties to and from specify the dependency property value in the beginning and end of the iteration. Using the property by, you can specify by how much the animation should change (obviously if you use the property by, the other two properties are redundant – the animation will simply increase the current value by the value specified in the property by). You can also specify at what point an animation should start, and how long it should last by using the BeginTime and Duration properties of the animation class. Since the animations control DPs of different types, there is a specific built-in animation class for every type that is likely to be animated. Animation names usually start with the name of the type. The following Silverlight simple animations are the most important ones:

    i.   DoubleAnimation: This animates a double DP (we used it previously to animate the RotationAngle DP of the SpinningControl object).

    ii. ColorAnimation: This animates color transitions.

    iii. PointAnimation: This animates Points, that is, pairs of double values.

- **Key frame animations**: These animations also allow us to specify property values at certain points between the beginning and the end of the iteration. Correspondingly, key frame animations do not have to, from, and by properties. Instead, such animations have the KeyFrames property – a collection that can be populated with objects of the key frame class. Key frame classes differ by the type of interpolation that they use in order to interpolate the value between the key frame times. There are Discrete, Linear, and Spline interpolations. The names of key frame classes are composed of the interpolation type, animation type (corresponding to the DP type), and KeyFrame suffix, for example, LinearDoubleKeyFrame. Key frame animation class names start with the interpolation type followed by the animation type and end with the UsingKeyFrames suffix. The most important key frame animations are:

  i.   DoubleAnimationUsingKeyFrames

  ii. ColorAnimationUsingKeyFrames

  iii. PointAnimationUsingKeyFrames

Attached properties

One constraint on the dependency properties is that they have to be defined within a class that uses them. In many cases, however, developers might want to add properties to an object of a predefined class without extending the class. WPF and Silverlight came up with a new concept that allows doing just that – **attached properties (APs)**. APs can be defined in some (usually static) class and can be used to attach properties to any object derived from a DependencyObject.

An attached property sample can be found in the SpinningWithAttachedPropertySample folder. To create your own sample, create a new project and add a C# file/class to it called AttachedProperties. Make this class static and use the propa snippet to create the RotateAngle attached property in it:

```csharp
#region RotationAngle attached Property
public static double GetRotationAngle(DependencyObject obj)
{
    return (double)obj.GetValue(RotationAngleProperty);
}

public static void SetRotationAngle(DependencyObject obj, double value)
    {
    obj.SetValue(RotationAngleProperty, value);
```

```
}

public static readonly DependencyProperty RotationAngleProperty =
DependencyProperty.RegisterAttached
(
    "RotationAngle",
    typeof(double),
    typeof(AttachedProperties),
    new PropertyMetadata(0.0)
);
#endregion RotationAngle attached Property
```

You can see that unlike dependency properties, the attached properties have two static accessor methods GetRotationAngle and SetRotationAngle.

Now we can animate this attached property within the MainPage.xaml file in a very similar way to animating the dependency property. In the following section, we show the regions of XAML code that are different from the dependency property code.

In our attached property animation project, we will define a Storyboard object in exactly the same way as we did for the dependency property, the only difference is that we cannot specify Storyboard.TargetProperty within XAML:

```
<UserControl.Resources>
        <Storyboard x:Key="RotationStoryboard"
                    Storyboard.TargetName="TheRotatingRectangle">
            <DoubleAnimation BeginTime="00:00:00"
                             Duration="00:00:01"
                             From="0"
                             To="360"
                             RepeatBehavior="Forever" />
        </Storyboard>
</UserControl.Resources>
```

Unfortunately, Silverlight does not allow a storyboard to reference a custom attached property in XAML. Due to this limitation, we are forced to add such a reference in the C# code-behind.

The following is the XAML definition of a spinning Rectangle. The only difference between this code and the DP-related code previously presented is that we are using the full path within parentheses to point to the attached property within the Binding definition:

```
<Rectangle x:Name="TheRotatingRectangle"
           Fill="Orange"
           Width="100"
```

```
            Height="30"
            RenderTransformOrigin="0.5,0.5">
    <Rectangle.RenderTransform>
        <RotateTransform
          Angle="{Binding
                Path=(SpinningWithAP:AttachedProperties.
  RotationAngle),
                Mode=OneWay,
                ElementName=TheRotatingRectangle}"/>
    </Rectangle.RenderTransform>
</Rectangle>
```

You can see that the visual element does not have to be a custom control, we can use an attached property on an element built into Silverlight – `Rectangle`.

Finally, as was previously stated, due to a Silverlight limitation, we have to specify the storyboard's `TargetProperty` within the C# code. We can do this in the `MainPage` constructor as shown in the following snippet:

```csharp
public MainPage()
{
    InitializeComponent();

    Storyboard rotationStoryboard =
        (Storyboard) this.Resources["RotationStoryboard"];

    Storyboard.SetTargetProperty
    (
    rotationStoryboard,
    new PropertyPath(AttachedProperties.RotationAngleProperty)
    );
}
```

Summary

This chapter has defined the building blocks for future discussion, namely dependency and attached properties, lookless controls, bindings, and storyboards. It gives an example of using the MS Expression Blend SDK interactivity functionality. All of these will be used throughout the book to build animations. It is assumed that the reader already has some knowledge of the aforementioned subjects and uses this chapter only as a refresher. For an in-depth treatment of these subjects, we provide the reader with references within the text.

The next chapter will build on this material to cover creating animation is Silverlight business applications.

2
Animations in Business Logic Silverlight Applications

When you build a Silverlight application, animations can play a large role in spicing it up, making it more user-friendly and intuitive. This chapter shows how to achieve this by employing the following techniques:

- Using `VisualStateManager` to animate custom controls
- Animating navigation transitions

Animating Silverlight controls

Silverlight provides many built-in controls. It also empowers the developers to create their own controls – so called custom controls. Even the built-in Silverlight controls can be fully re-styled with all of their visual parts replaced by the designer. In the following sections, you will see how to use the `VisualStateManager` concept in order to provide custom animations for a built-in Silverlight button and later for a custom button-like control.

Tools for animating controls

Here is some bad news and good news for the WPF developers: the bad news – Silverlight does not have a built-in property or data triggers to trigger a visual change within a style or a template; the good news – the MS Expression Blend SDK functionality to a large degree mitigates this deficiency by providing classes to replace missing triggers. `DataTriggers` can detect a change of property within a control and fire, for example, `ChangePropertyAction` – which can trigger some visual property change, or `ControlStoryboardAction`, which can start, stop, or pause a storyboard, similar to the WPF triggers.

The trigger functionality is perfect when it comes to instantaneous visual change (and `DataTrigger`/`ChangePropertyAction` combination is very useful for that), but when it comes to animations, keeping track of all storyboards invoked on different triggers (in order to stop them when a different trigger is fired) might be tedious. The Silverlight team has come up with a functionality that helps with that. It invokes and stops correct animations based on the visual states of the controls. This functionality is called `VisualStateManager` and it will be explained and extensively used throughout the following section.

Animating a built-in button

The code that we describe in this section is located under the `AnimatingButtonStates.sln` solution.

A Silverlight button has the following mouse-driven states:

- **Normal**
- **MouseOver**
- **Pressed**

Note that there might be more states to a fully functioning button, for example, there is also a **Disabled** state, but whether a button is disabled or not usually does not depend on mouse movements or positions, it does not have to be animated, and we do not describe it here. Our purpose in this section is not to create a fully functioning button, but rather to demonstrate some generic concepts for re-styling a control and providing custom animations for it.

Let's create a Silverlight project containing a single page with the button in its center. The following is the resulting XAML code of the main page:

```
<UserControl
    x:Class="AnimatingButtonStates.MainPage"
    xmlns="http://schemas.microsoft.com/winfx/2006/xaml/presentation"
    xmlns:x="http://schemas.microsoft.com/winfx/2006/xaml">
    <Grid x:Name="LayoutRoot" Background="White">
        <Button Width="100"
                Height="25"
                Background="LightGray"
                Content="Press Me" />
    </Grid>
</UserControl>
```

We want to re-style this button completely, modifying it shape, border, colors, and creating custom animations for the transition between states.

Now, we'll create a very simple custom template for the button by changing the button code to the following code:

```
<!-- Here we provide custom button template -->
<Button>   <Button.Template>
    <ControlTemplate TargetType="Button">
        <Grid x:Name="TopLevelButtonGrid">
            <!--Button Border-->
            <Border x:Name="ButtonBorder"
                    HorizontalAlignment="Stretch"
                    VerticalAlignment="Stretch"
                    CornerRadius="5"
                    Background="{TemplateBinding Background}"
                    BorderBrush="{TemplateBinding BorderBrush}"
                    BorderThickness="{TemplateBinding
BorderThickness}">
            </Border>

            <!-- button content is placed here-->
            <ContentPresenter HorizontalAlignment="Center"
                              VerticalAlignment="Center" />
        </Grid>
    </ControlTemplate>
  </Button.Template>
<Button>
```

If we run the code, as it is, we shall be able to see the button and its **Press Me** content, but the button will not react visually to mouse over or press events. That is because once we replace the button's template we will have to provide our own solution to the visual changes for different button states.

Now, let's discuss how we want the button to look in the different states and how we want it to handle the transitions between states.

When the mouse is over the button, we want a blue border to appear. The animation to achieve this can be fast or even instantaneous.

When the button is pressed, we want it to scale down significantly and we want the button to scale up and down several times, each time with lower amplitude before achieving a steady pressed state.

Note that the control template developers and designers usually try to avoid changing colors within animations (they are considered to be more complex and less intuitive); instead, they try to achieve color-changing effects by changing opacities of several template parts. So to change the border to *blue* on mouse over, let's create another border element MouseOverBorder with blue BorderBrush, and non-zero BorderThickness within the control template. At normal state, its opacity property will be 0, and it will be completely transparent. When the state of the button changes to MouseOver, the opacity of this border will change to 1.

After we add the MouseOverBorder element together with the visual state manager functionality, the resulting template code will look as follows:

```
<Button>
  <Button.Template>
    <ControlTemplate TargetType="Button">
      <Grid x:Name="TopLevelButtonGrid">
        <VisualStateManager.VisualStateGroups>
          <VisualStateGroup>
            <VisualStateGroup.Transitions>
              <!-- duration for the MouseOver animation is set
                   here to 0.2 seconds -->
              <VisualTransition To="MouseOver"
                                GeneratedDuration="0:0:0.2" />
            </VisualStateGroup.Transitions>
            <VisualState x:Name="Normal" />
            <VisualState x:Name="MouseOver">
              <VisualState.Storyboard>
                <Storyboard>
                  <!--animation performed when the
                      button gets into "MouseOver"
                      State-->
                  <DoubleAnimation Storyboard.
                      TargetName="MouseOverBorder"
                             Storyboard.TargetProperty="Opacity"
                             To="1" />
                </Storyboard>
              </VisualState.Storyboard>
            </VisualState>
          </VisualStateGroup>
        </VisualStateManager.VisualStateGroups>

        <!--Button Border-->
        <Border x:Name="ButtonBorder"
                HorizontalAlignment="Stretch"
```

```
                VerticalAlignment="Stretch"
                CornerRadius="5"
                Background="{TemplateBinding Background}"
                BorderBrush="{TemplateBinding BorderBrush}"
                BorderThickness="{TemplateBinding BorderThickness}">
       </Border>

       <!--MouseOverBorder has opacity 0 normally.
           Only when the mouse moves over the button,
           the opacity is changed to 1-->
       <Border x:Name="MouseOverBorder"
               HorizontalAlignment="Stretch"
               VerticalAlignment="Stretch"
               CornerRadius="5"
               BorderBrush="Blue"
               BorderThickness="2"
               Opacity="0">
       </Border>

       <!-- button content is placed here-->
       <ContentPresenter HorizontalAlignment="Center"
                         VerticalAlignment="Center" />
     </Grid>
   </ControlTemplate>
  </Button.Template>
</Button>
```

Now, if we start the application, we'll see that the border of the button becomes blue, if the mouse pointer is placed over it, and returns to its usual color when the mouse pointer is moved away from the button, as shown in the following screenshot:

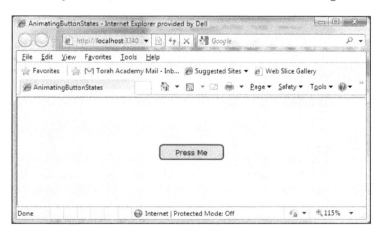

The next step is to animate the pressed state.

To achieve this, we add a `ScaleTransform` object to the top-level grid of the button's template:

```
<ControlTemplate TargetType="Button">
    <Grid x:Name="TopLevelButtonGrid"
          RenderTransformOrigin="0.5,0.5">
        <Grid.RenderTransform>
            <!-- scale transform is used to shrink the button
                 when it is pressed -->
            <ScaleTransform x:Name="OnPressedScaleTransform"
                            ScaleX="1"
                            ScaleY="1" />
        </Grid.RenderTransform>
    . . .
```

The purpose of the `ScaleTransform` object is to shrink the button once it is pressed. Originally, its `ScaleX` and `ScaleY` parameters are set to 1, while the animation that starts when the button is pressed changes them to 0.5.

This animation is defined within `VisualState` defined as `Pressed`:

```
<VisualStateGroup>
    . . .
    <VisualState x:Name="Pressed">
        <VisualState.Storyboard>
            <Storyboard>
                <!-- animation performed when the
                     button gets into "Pressed"
                     State will scale down the button
                     by a factor of 0.5 in both dimensions -->
                <DoubleAnimation Storyboard.TargetProperty="ScaleX"
                        Storyboard.TargetName="TheScaleTransform"
                                 To="0.5" />
                <DoubleAnimation Storyboard.TargetProperty="ScaleY"
                        Storyboard.TargetName="TheScaleTransform"
                                 To="0.5" />
            </Storyboard>
        </VisualState.Storyboard>
    </VisualState>
    . . .
</VisualStateGroup>
```

`VisualState` defines the animation storyboard to be triggered once the button switches to the `Pressed` state.

We can also add `VisualStateTransition` to the `VisualStateGroup` element's `Transition` property:

```
<VisualStateManager.VisualStateGroups>
    <VisualStateGroup>
        <VisualStateGroup.Transitions>
            . . .
            <VisualTransition To="Pressed"
                            GeneratedDuration="0:0:0.5">
                <VisualTransition.GeneratedEasingFunction>
                    <!-- elastic ease will provide a few attenuating
                        bounces before the pressed button reaches
                        a steady state -->
                    <ElasticEase />
                </VisualTransition.GeneratedEasingFunction>
            </VisualTransition>
        </VisualStateGroup.Transitions>
        . . .
    </VisuateStateGroup>
</VisualStateManager.VisualStateGroups>
```

`VisualTransition` elements allow us to modify the animation behavior depending on what the original and final states of the transition are. It has properties such as `From` and `To` for the purpose of specifying the original and final states. In our case, we set only its `To` property to `Pressed`, which means that it applies to transit from any state to the `Pressed` state. `VisualTransition` sets the duration of the animation to `0.5` second and adds the `ElasticEase` easing function to it, which results in the button size bouncing effect.

Once we started talking about easing functions, we can explain in detail how they work, and give examples of other easing functions.

Easing functions provide a way to modify Silverlight (and WPF) animations. A good article describing easing functions can be found at `http://tinyurl.com/arbitrarypathanimations`. The easing formula presented in this article is:

```
v = (V2 - V1)/T * f(t/T) + V1
```

Here `v` is the resulting animation value, `t` is the time parameter, `T` is the time period in question (either time between two frames in an animation with frames or time between the `To` and `From` values in the case of a simple animation), `V2` and `V1` are the animation values at the end and beginning of the animation correspondingly at the absence of easing, and `f` is the easing function. In the previous formula, we assumed a linear animation (not a spline one).

There are a bunch of built-in easing functions that come together with the Silverlight framework, for example, BackEase, BounceEase, CircleEase, and so on. For a comprehensive list of built-in easing functions, please check the following website: http://tinyurl.com/silverlighteasing. Most easing functions have parameters described on this website. As an exercise you can change the easing function in the previous VisualTransition XAML code, modify its parameters, and observe the changes in button animation.

Creating and animating custom button control

In the previous subsection, we re-built a template for a built-in button using the VisualStateManager functionality to provide custom animations between the states. An attentive reader might have noticed, though, that the button states that we used – Normal, MouseOver, and Pressed had come with the built-in button functionality – we only provided ways to visualize the transitions between those states, but did not define the states themselves.

In this subsection, we will build a custom control behaving exactly like the previous button. We will show how to define the aforementioned visual states on a custom control built from scratch.

The code corresponding to this subsection is located under the AnimatingCustomButton.sln solution. Most of the code is the same as the one for the built-in button. The only difference is that we use the CustomButton class in place of Button that we used in the previous subsection. CustomButton is defined within the CustomButton.cs file. You can see from the following code that it is derived from the ContentControl class and not from the Button class. It defines two Boolean dependency properties, IsPressed and IsMouseOver, corresponding to the Pressed and MouseOver states. It defines the handlers for the mouse events that set those properties to the correct values. It also has a function, SetVisualState, that is called whenever the IsPressed or IsMouseOver property changes. It uses the VisualStateManager.GoToState function to set the correct visual state on the CustomButton control:

```
/// <summary>
/// this function sets the visual state
/// depending on the values of the properties
/// IsPressed and IsMouseOver
/// </summary>
void SetVisualState()
{
    string stateName = "Normal";

    if (IsPressed)
```

```
        stateName = "Pressed";
    else if (IsMouseOver)
        stateName = "MouseOver";

    VisualStateManager.GoToState(this, stateName, true);
}
```

Animating navigation panels

Almost any application provides a way to switch (navigate) between different screens. Good navigation functionality should give the users ideas of whether it was a forward or backward movement, and give hints of how to move to the previously shown screens. This section describes ways of creating intuitive navigation functionality using animations.

Let's assume that we are moving from screen to screen mostly in a bidirectional way either forward (to the right) or backwards (to the left). Under a forward move, it will make sense to show the new panel coming from the right and the old panel disappearing on the left-hand side of the application. Under a backward movement, the panels will move in the opposite direction. A more involved animation can result in a page-like movement with the previous page being flipped away, and a new page turned open for the view.

The NavigationAnimations.sln sample shows how to create such animations. The sample is built around TransitioningContentControl – an open source control provided by Microsoft Silverlight Toolkit specifically to help with navigation animation. MS Toolkit is a bulky piece of software to install, so in order to help you avoid installing all of it, we have provided an MSLayoutToolkit project under the SAMPLES directory containing only the TransitioningContentControl functionality. If you do not want to install the whole MS Toolkit, you have to reference this project instead.

More information on using TransitioningContentControl for navigations can be obtained in a phone article by Jeff Brand at http://tinyurl.com/silverlighttransitions. The animation to imitate page flipping was borrowed from that article and modified to flip the pages horizontally (Jeff's animation does it vertically).

The NavigationAnimations sample is built as a pure **Model-View-ViewModel (MVVM)** application. For detailed explanations about the MVVM pattern, please read http://tinyurl.com/mvvmsimple.

The view models are represented by the classes ScreenVM and NavigationVM. The ScreenVM class has just one integer property ScreenNumber, which is used for demo purposes. We only allow our individual screens to differ from each other by a number:

```
public class ScreenVM
{
    public int ScreenNumber { get; set; }
}
```

The NavigationVM class contains a collection of TheScreens of ScreenVM objects. We populate this collection within the class constructor with three screens – screen numbers varying from 1 to 3:

```
public class NavigationVM
{
    . . .
    public List<ScreenVM> TheScreens { get; private set; }

    public NavigationVM()
    {
        TheScreens = new List<ScreenVM>();

        AddScreen(1);
        AddScreen(2);
        AddScreen(3);

        . . .
    }
    . . .
}
```

The NavigationVM class implements the INotifyPropertyChanged interface. INotifyPropertyChanged provides the PropertyChanged event. Silverlight bindings register for this event and update the binding target value whenever the event is fired, with the argument that matches the name of the binding source property. Thus, all we need to do is refresh the binding target so as to fire the PropertyChanged event within the code at proper moments. The OnPropertyChanged function facilitates just that.

The CurrentScreenIdx property is used to point to the index of the current screen within the TheScreens collection, as shown in the following snippet:

```
int _currentScreenIdx = 0;
int CurrentScreenIdx
{
    get
```

```
    {
        return _currentScreenIdx;
    }

    set
    {
        _currentScreenIdx = value;

        . . .

    }
}
```

The CurrentScreen property returns the ScreenVM object from the TheScreens collection corresponding to CurrentScreenIdx:

```
public ScreenVM CurrentScreen
{
    get
    {
        if (CurrentScreenIdx < 0)
            return null;

        return TheScreens[CurrentScreenIdx];
    }
}
```

The TransitionName property allows the view model to change TransitionName of the visual TransitionContentControl object. We will talk more about this when describing the visual code.

The MoveToNext and MoveToPrevious functions simply change the current screen to the next or the previous screen respectively. They also choose the correct transition to be performed depending on whether we are moving forward or backwards:

```
public void MoveToNext()
{
    TransitionName = "LeftSwingTransition";
    CurrentScreenIdx++;
}

. . .

public void MoveToPrevious()
{
    TransitionName = "RightSwingTransition";
    CurrentScreenIdx--;
}
```

The CanMoveToNext and CanMoveToPrevious properties simply state if there is a screen after or before the current screen:

```
public bool CanMoveToNext
{
    get
    {
        return CurrentScreenIdx < (TheScreens.Count - 1);
    }
}

public bool CanMoveToPrevious
{
    get
    {
        return CurrentScreenIdx > 0;
    }
}
```

We use these two properties to set *forward* and *backwards* buttons to enabled or disabled in our view.

Note that Bindings to CurrentScreen, CanMoveToNext, and CanMoveToPrevous properties are updated when CurrentScreenIdx changes via calls to OnPropertyChanged:

```
/// <summary>
/// specifies the current screen's index
/// within TheScreens collection
/// </summary>
int _currentScreenIdx = 0;
int CurrentScreenIdx
{
    get
    {
        return _currentScreenIdx;
    }

    set
    {
        _currentScreenIdx = value;

        // fires PropertyChanged events to
        // the binding targets for all the properties
        // that might change due to CurrentScreenIdx
        // change
        OnPropertyChanged("CurrentScreen");
        OnPropertyChanged("CanMoveToNext");
```

```
                OnPropertyChanged("CanMoveToPrevious");
        }
    }
```

Now let's turn our attention to the *view* (the visual code).

All the visual XAML code is located within the `MainPage.xaml` file.

At the top of the logical tree (the tree of elements as they are arranged in the XAML file), there is a `LayoutRoot` grid panel. Note that its `DataContext` property is connected to the `TheNavigationVM` object defined as a resource within the same `MainPage.xaml` file:

```
<Grid x:Name="LayoutRoot"
        Background="Yellow"
        DataContext="{StaticResource TheNavigationVM}">
```

`DataContext` propagates down the logical tree to every element defined within the tree (unless there are some elements that change it or unless we have `ItemsControl` within the tree – which is not the case in our code). `DataContext` provides a default binding source so that the binding can be defined only by `Path`.

The layout of the application is very simple, most of the window is occupied by the screen viewer – represented by `TransitioningContentControl`, while there are navigation buttons at the bottom of the screen; the one on the right – for moving forward, the one on the left – for moving backwards, as is shown in the following screenshot:

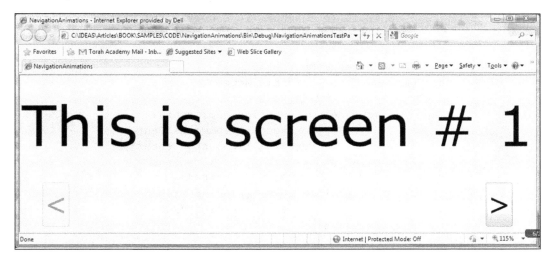

The *forward* and *backwards* buttons call the `NavigationVM` class' `MoveToNext` and `MoveToPrevious` methods, respectively, to change the current screen object. The buttons' `IsEnabled` properties are bound to the `CanMoveToNext` and `CanMoveToPrevious` properties, respectively, so that the *forward* button is disabled when the `CurrentScreen` points to the last screen of the `NavigationVM` object and the *backwards* button is disabled when `CurrentScreen` points to the first screen.

The centrepiece of the view is `TransitioningContentControl` from MS Layout Toolkit since it is in charge of navigation animations. `TransitioningContentControl` triggers navigation animation when its `Content` property changes.

Here is the how `TransitioningContentControl` is defined within XAML code:

```
<!-- TransitioningContentControl is in charge of the navigation
animations -->
<msLayoutToolkit:TransitioningContentControl
    x:Name="TheTransitioningContentControl"
    Template="{StaticResource TransitioningContentControlTemplate}"
    Transition="{Binding Path=TransitionName}"
    Content="{Binding Path=CurrentScreen}"
    HorizontalAlignment="Stretch"
    VerticalAlignment="Stretch"
    HorizontalContentAlignment="Stretch"
    VerticalContentAlignment="Stretch">
    <msLayoutToolkit:TransitioningContentControl.ContentTemplate>
        <!-- ContentTemplate of the TransitioningContentControl
                Converts the non-visual Content into a visual
                control. In our case it converts the ScreenVM object
                into a panel containing
                the Text "This is screen # " followed by
                the ScreenNumber -->
        <DataTemplate DataType="this:ScreenVM">
            <Grid Background="AliceBlue">
                <StackPanel Orientation="Horizontal"
                            HorizontalAlignment="Center"
                            VerticalAlignment="Center">
                    <TextBlock Text="This is screen # "
                                FontSize="100"/>
                    <TextBlock Text="{Binding ScreenNumber}"
                                FontSize="100"/>
                </StackPanel>
            </Grid>
        </DataTemplate>
    </msLayoutToolkit:TransitioningContentControl.ContentTemplate>
</msLayoutToolkit:TransitioningContentControl>
```

Note that the `TransitionName` property of `TransitioningContentControl` is bound to the `TransitionName` property of the `NavigationVM` data context object. This property controls the type of animation that we are playing. When we press the *forward* button, the *forward* animation should be played, and pressing the *backwards* button should cause the *backwards* animation to play.

The `Content` property of `TransitioningContentControl` is set to the `CurrentScreen` property of its `NavigationVM` data context object. `CurrentScreen` is represented by a non-visual object of type `ScreenVM`.

The `ContentTemplate` property of `TransitioningContentControl` is needed to convert the non-visual content into a visual object:

```
<DataTemplate DataType="this:ScreenVM">
    <Grid Background="AliceBlue">
        <StackPanel Orientation="Horizontal"
                    HorizontalAlignment="Center"
                    VerticalAlignment="Center">
            <TextBlock Text="This is screen # "
                    FontSize="100"/>
            <TextBlock Text="{Binding ScreenNumber}"
                    FontSize="100"/>
        </StackPanel>
    </Grid>
</DataTemplate>
```

As you can see, this data template results in huge text: **This is screen #**, followed by the screen number in the middle of the screen.

The core of the `TransitioningContentControl` animation functionality resides in its control template defined within the `UserControl.Resources` section at the top of the file. The template's name is `TransitioningContentControlTemplate` and as you can see, it is quite large. So let's try to dissect it here.

The outer border is just a frame for containing the rest of the control – not a very consequential part.

Within that outer border, we can see the Visual State definitions that actually define the transition animation storyboards and a grid panel containing two `ContentPresenter` objects with the names `PreviousContentPresenterSite` and `CurrentContentPresenterSite`.

During the navigation animation, the `PreviousContentPresenterSite` content presenter represents the old content that is being replaced while `CurrentContentPresenterSite` represents the new content replacing the old one. Note that outside of the navigation animation, only the `CurrentContentPresenterSite` content is visible, we do not care what the other `ContentPresenter` contains:

```
<Grid>
    <!-- during the navigation animation this ContentPresenter
        contains the old content that's being replaced.
         Outside the navigation boundaries, this ContentPresenter
         is not visible and we simply do not care what it
         contains-->
    <ContentPresenter
        x:Name="PreviousContentPresentationSite"
        Content="{x:Null}"
        ContentTemplate="{TemplateBinding ContentTemplate}"
        HorizontalAlignment="{TemplateBinding
HorizontalContentAlignment}"
        VerticalAlignment="{TemplateBinding
VerticalContentAlignment}">
        . . .
    </ContentPresenter>

    <!-- during the navigation animation this ContentPresenter
            contains the new content that's replacing the old one.
            Outside the navigation boundaries, this ContentPresenter
            is visible contain the same content as the
            TransitionContentControl's Content property -->
    <ContentPresenter
        x:Name="CurrentContentPresentationSite"
        Content="{x:Null}"
        ContentTemplate="{TemplateBinding ContentTemplate}"
        HorizontalAlignment="{TemplateBinding
HorizontalContentAlignment}"
        VerticalAlignment="{TemplateBinding
VerticalContentAlignment}">
        . . .
    </ContentPresenter>
</Grid>
```

When the content of the `TransitioningContentControl` object changes, the storyboard of the visual state whose name matches the string in the `TransitioningContentControl` object's `TransitionName` property, will be called to manage the transition.

There are the following visual states within the template: Normal, RightSlideTransition, LeftSlideTransition, RightSwingTransition, and LeftSwingTransition. Any of the TransitioningContentControl object's template should have a Normal state, which kicks in when there are no animations going on. All it usually does is sets PreviousContentPresenterSite to be invisible.

The **slide** animations are in charge of the sliding navigation, while the **swing** animations are in charge of the page-like navigation.

To use slide animations, change the NavigationVM class' MoveToNext and MoveToPrevious functions to set TransitionName, the View Model property to LeftSlideTransition and RightSlideTransition, respectively, before modifying CurrentScreenIdx:

```
public void MoveToNext()
{
    TransitionName = "LeftSlideTransition";
    CurrentScreenIdx++;
}

public void MoveToPrevious()
{
    TransitionName = "RightSlideTransition";
    CurrentScreenIdx--;
}
```

To use the page-like navigation, change TransitionName to be set to LeftSwingTransition and RightSwingTransition in the same places.

```
public void MoveToNext()
{
    TransitionName = "LeftSwingTransition";
    CurrentScreenIdx++;
}

public void MoveToPrevious()
{
    TransitionName = "RightSwingTransition";
    CurrentScreenIdx--;
}
```

The following is a screenshot of the window in the midst of `LeftSlideTransition` with screen 1 being replaced by screen 2:

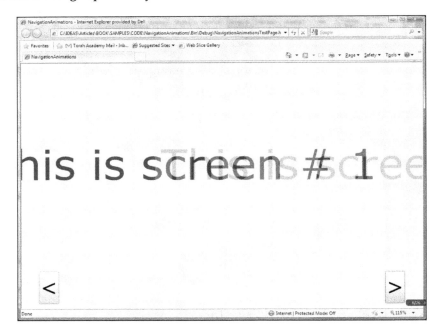

And the following is the screenshot of page-like `LeftSwingTransition` navigation:

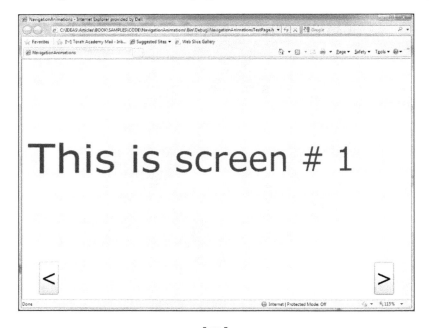

Summary

Using button state animations as an example, we saw in this chapter how to change the transition animations on a control, whether it is a Silverlight built-in control or a custom control.

We have also seen how to animate the navigation between pages in a Silverlight application and described `TransitionContentControl` in detail.

The next chapter will describe generating and animating random fields imitating natural processes, such as clouds or fire.

3
Creating Animated Textures

Silverlight provides functionality for creating powerful animation including imitation of different natural processes, for example, clouds, fire, and so on. This chapter presents implementation of the Perlin noise algorithm in Silverlight and presents samples for using Perlin noise to generate clouds and fire visual effects.

Background on Perlin noise

Here we provide a background on Perlin noise and explain the Perlin noise algorithm in detail.

A bit of history

Perlin noise is probably the most popular algorithm for generating random textures. Perlin noise was invented in 1985 by Ken Perlin, a professor at NYU and among other things was used for creating animations for several movies including Oscar winning Tron and many others. Here is the URL to a talk by Ken Perlin, detailing what has been achieved using Perlin noise: `http://www.noisemachine.com/talk1/index.html`.

The big advantage of using Perlin noise is that even though it is random, the pixels next to each other are still correlated – just the way they are in natural textures.

Perlin noise algorithm

Noise is a function that maps any point in a one, two, three, or more dimensional space into a real number. Usually we are only interested in noise that cannot grow infinitely high or low, so without the loss of generality we can assume that our noise maps a point into a real number within a finite range.

There are two parts to the Perlin noise calculation algorithm (the meaning of these parts will be explained shortly):

- **Calculating noise at one octave (frequency)**: We call it **basic Perlin noise**. This is the core of the Perlin noise algorithm and is well explained at `http://tinyurl.com/basicperlintheory`.

- **Calculating multi-scale Perlin Noise**: This is done by summing up the noises produced by the first part calculated at different octaves (or frequencies) multiplied by appropriate amplitude factors. This part is common to fractal noise techniques not only to Perlin noise. Good explanations of this part can be found at `http://tinyurl.com/multiscaleperlin`.

Let's start by explaining the second part and after that, we will dive into the first.

Multi-scale Perlin noise

There is a notion of frequency in basic Perlin noise calculation – the higher frequencies produce a more refined noise, while the lower frequencies produce a more slowly changing one. We can write the basic Perlin noise function as `BasicPerlinNoise<frequency>(x)` – here `frequency` is just a function parameter, not a template and `x` is a pixel in a one-dimensional space. The description of **Multi-scale Perlin noise** previously mentioned simply states that the total Perlin noise is calculated according the following formula:

```
MultiscalePerlinNoise (x) =
(BasicPerlinNoise<frequency>(x) + BasicPerlinNoise<2*frequency
>(x) * persistence + BasicPerlinNoise<2 * 2 * frequency>(x) *
persistence * persistence + ...) * amplitude
```

Or using summation notations:

`MultiscalePerlinNoise (x) =`

$$amplitude * \sum_{Octave=0}^{TotalOctaves} persistence^{Octave} * BasicPerlinNoise<frequency * 2^{Octave}>(x)$$

In other words, we take basic Perlin noise at some frequency, then take basic Perlin noise at double the original frequency and multiply it by a **persistence** factor, continue doing it until we reach the number of octaves we want, sum up the results, and multiply it by the **amplitude** factor.

As was stated in the previous section, this procedure of summing up noises at different frequencies is not unique for Perlin noise but is also used for other fractal noises. Its purpose is to make noise look more natural as many natural processes are changing at different frequencies, not at a single one.

Basic Perlin noise

Now we are going to explain how to produce basic Perlin noise. First let's talk about one-dimensional noise as the simplest case and later we will generalize it to multiple dimensions.

To construct basic Perlin noise, divide the one-dimensional noise domain into intervals of some length L. Assign random one-dimensional unit gradient vectors to every point at which two intervals meet. Since all the gradient vectors are of unit length, there can be only one of two vectors assigned at each point – the one pointing to the left or the one pointing to the right.

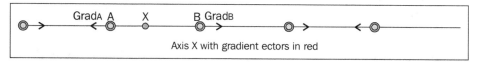

Axis X with gradient ectors in red

At every point within the interval, calculate the noise via the following algorithm:

1. Assume that we want to calculate noise at point X lying between interval points A and B. Assume that gradient vectors at points A and B are GradA and GradB.

2. We calculate the gradient vector influences Ax and Bx at point X by taking inner products of the corresponding gradient vectors with vectors AX and BX:

    Ax = <GradA, AX>

    Bx= <GradB, BX>

 Just a reminder – the inner vector product equals to the product of the norms of the vectors multiplied by the cosine of the angle between them. In orthonormal terms, it is equivalent to the dot product.

3. Now calculate the noise value at X by averaging values Ax and Bx proportionate to its distance from X. The averaging function is usually not linear, but a smooth function with zero derivatives at points A and B.

Usually for convenience sake without loss of generality, it is assumed that the one-dimensional domain is split into intervals of length 1. A and B are some integer points with B = A + 1 and X is a real point between them. It is also assumed that the output noise result lies within the 0 to 1 interval (if we need larger intervals or negative values, we can also shift and scale the output to obtain the result we need).

Frequency, used to create multi-scale noise, is inversely proportional to the number of real pixels within the integer interval of the algorithm. The more pixels we have between two adjacent integer locations, the smoother the noise is going to be.

We can easily generalize the result for two and more dimensions. For an explanation of the two-dimensional noise, we refer to `http://tinyurl.com/basicperlintheory`.

Perlin noise algorithm implementation

Our Perlin noise Silverlight implementation is based on those described at `http://tinyurl.com/perlinalgo` and `http://tinyurl.com/perlinalgosl` with some performance improvements.

The code is located under the `PerlinNoise.csproj` project (it is a Silverlight shared library – not an executable) within the `PerlinNoiseImpl.cs` file. To open the project one can open for example: the `PerlinClouds.sln` solution.

We implemented 3D Perlin noise since Perlin himself stated that only 3D noise results should feature in realistic images. Basic Perlin noise is produced by the function `GetBasicPerlinNoise` while Multi-scale Perlin noise is produced by the `GetMultiscalePerlinNoise` function that uses `GetBasicPerlinNoise` to produce the resulting multi-scale noise based on the following formula:

```
MultiscalePerlinNoise (x) =
```

$$\text{amplitude} * \sum_{Octave=0}^{TotalOctaves} \text{persistence}^{Octave} * \text{BasicPerlinNoise}<\text{frequency} * 2^{Octave}>(x)$$

The code is well documented and explained by the comments within it.

The following are some explanations regarding the `GetBasicPerlinNoise` function:

- The `GetBasicPerlinNoise` function calculates 3D basic Perlin noise. Its input arguments x, y, and z correspond to the point coordinates within 3D space. The function returns a noise value at this point:

  ```
  float GetBasicPerlinNoise(float x, float y, float z)
  ```

- As we discussed in the previous section, the function approximates the value at each point based on the values at integer lattice, so we round down the values x, y, and z to the nearest smaller integers:

  ```
  int intX = (int)x;
  int intY = (int)y;
  int intZ = (int)z;
  ```

The noise value at (x, y, z) point will be determined by the gradient value at the points of the integer cube starting at (intX, intY, intZ) point and ending at (intX+1, intY+1, intZ+1) point.

At this point, we are only interested in distances between (x, y, z) point and the vertices of the integer cube, so we can move the coordinate origin into (intX, intY, intZ) point and change x, y, and z values accordingly:

```
x -= intX;
y -= intY;
z -= intZ;
```

- We assign gradients to the points of the cube based on the random gradients array:

```
// the names of the variables below correspond to
// location of the gradient for example.
// gradXYZ   is a gradient at point XYZ
// gradX1Y1Zy is a gradient at point X + 1, Y + 1, Z + 1
int gradXY = gradients[X] + Y;
int gradXYZ = gradients[gradXY] + Z;

int gradXY1Z = gradients[gradXY + 1] + Z;

int gradX1Y = gradients[X + 1] + Y;
int gradX1YZ = gradients[gradX1Y] + Z;
int gradX1Y1Z = gradients[gradX1Y + 1] + Z;

int gradXYZ1 = gradients[gradXYZ + 1];
int gradX1YZ1 = gradients[gradX1YZ + 1];
int gradXY1Z1 = gradients[gradXY1Z + 1];
int gradX1Y1Z1 = gradients[gradX1Y1Z + 1];
```

- We calculate the inner products between each gradient vector and the vector from the corresponding vertex to (x, y, z) point:

```
// note that when here we use X + 1 point and pass x-1 as X
argument.
// this is because the vector from X + 1 point to x is given by x
- 1
// formula.
float innerProductX1YZ =
    InnerProduct(gradients[gradX1YZ], x - 1, y, z);
float innerProductXY1Z =
    InnerProduct(gradients[gradXY1Z], x, y - 1, z);
float innerProductX1Y1Z =
    InnerProduct(gradients[gradX1Y1Z], x - 1, y - 1, z);
```

```
float innerProductXYZ1 =
    InnerProduct(gradXYZ1, x, y, z - 1);
float innerProductX1YZ1 =
    InnerProduct(gradX1YZ1, x - 1, y, z - 1);
float innerProductXY1Z1 =
    InnerProduct(gradXY1Z1, x, y - 1, z - 1);
float innerProductX1Y1Z1 =
    InnerProduct(gradX1Y1Z1, x - 1, y - 1, z - 1);
```

- Finally we use the interpolation function `Fade` and the approximation function `Lerp` to determine the nose value at (x, y, z) point.

As we are dealing with three dimensions, we are using cubes instead of intervals. We find the random gradient at the cube vertices by using an array called `gradients` of random integers from 0 to 255 according to the following formula suggested by Perlin:

```
G[x, y, z] = gradients[x + gradients[y + gradients[z]]]
```

Here x, y, and z are integers from 0 to 255 (in order to adapt this formula for any set of integers, one can pass the integer values mod 256 to the formula).

Note that `gradients` array has length of 512 and has a set of random numbers between 0 and 255 repeated twice within it. This is to avoid the extra *mod* operations since, for example, `y + gradient[z]` can be greater than 255, but cannot be greater than 511.

ImageProcessingLibrary

We also use a project called `ImageProcessingLibrary` for generating moving images. It consists of several utility classes facilitating changing and retrieving colors:

- `DoubleColor` is a central class within the project. It contains information about R, G, B, and A bytes of a color using double precision variables (instead of bytes) to store them. Having these values stored as doubles makes it easier to manipulate them. The class also provides conversion functions between itself and the `System.Windows.Media.Color` class. It also provides a function to convert an object of the `DoubleColor` type to `int`.

- The `ColorUtils` class provides a bunch of extension methods facilitating changing colors (adding two colors, multiplying a color by a scalar, blending two colors, and so on).

- The `ColorMap` class provides a way to set a map between the colors we want to use and real numbers from within the 0 to 1 range.

Cloud simulation

Here we apply the Perlin noise and image manipulation algorithms previously described to obtain a simulation of the moving clouds.

The code is located under the `PerlinClouds` project.

One can see that the `MainPage.xaml` file is very simple; it contains only an image to be filled with the clouds.

```
<UserControl
    x:Class="PerlinClouds.MainPage"
    xmlns="http://schemas.microsoft.com/winfx/2006/xaml/presentation"
    xmlns:x="http://schemas.microsoft.com/winfx/2006/xaml"
    xmlns:d="http://schemas.microsoft.com/expression/blend/2008"
    xmlns:mc="http://schemas.openxmlformats.org/markup-
compatibility/2006"
    mc:Ignorable="d"
    d:DesignHeight="300"
    d:DesignWidth="400">

    <Grid Width="500"
        Height="400"
        Background="White">
      <!-- image to be filled with moving clouds -->
      <Image x:Name="PerlinNoiseImage"
            Stretch="UniformToFill" />
    </Grid>
</UserControl>
```

The code-behind located in the `MainPage.xaml.cs` file is more interesting – this is where we use all of the functionality from the libraries to generate the image.

The constructor of the `MainPage` class sets the noise parameters, creates the `WriteableMap` object to be populated by the noise pixels as the image source, and sets `ColorMap` for the sky and clouds:

```
public MainPage()
{
    InitializeComponent();

    // create PerlinNoiseImpl object
    _perlinNoiseImpl = new PerlinNoiseImpl();

    // set perlin noise multiscale parameters
    _perlinNoiseImpl.Amplitude = 1.2f;
```

```
_perlinNoiseImpl.NumberOctaves = 5;
_perlinNoiseImpl.Frequency = 0.006f;
_perlinNoiseImpl.Persistence = 0.4f;

//create writeable bitmap, ie. the source
// for the image within which one can modify the pixels
_writeableBitmap = new WriteableBitmap(200, 150);

// make the writeable bitmap to be the source
// for the image
PerlinNoiseImage.Source = _writeableBitmap;

// create a colormap for fast blending of sky and cloud colors
_colorMap = new ColorMap(skyColor, cloudColor);

// recalculate the image every time it is rendered
// by silverlight
CompositionTarget.Rendering += CompositionTarget_Rendering;
}
```

The function that actually generates the image is `CompositionTarget_Rendering`. It is called every time Silverlight renders the window. The function changes the noise parameters to create an illusion of moving clouds, calculates the noise value for each image pixel within `WriteableBitmap`, and forces the image refresh by calling `writeableBitmap.Invalidate()`. The following is how the function looks:

```
void CompositionTarget_Rendering(object sender, EventArgs e)
{
    // set offsets - make the clouds move and change
    for (int octaveIdx = 0;
         octaveIdx < _perlinNoiseImpl.NumberOctaves;
         octaveIdx++)
    {
        // the clouds move mainly along X axis
        _perlinNoiseImpl.OctaveOffsets[octaveIdx].XOffset += 1;
        // and a little a long y axis
        _perlinNoiseImpl.OctaveOffsets[octaveIdx].YOffset += 0.2f;

        // changes along z axis provide a visual effect corresponding
        // to the clouds changing shapes as they move
        _perlinNoiseImpl.OctaveOffsets[octaveIdx].ZOffset += 0.5f;
    }

    int z = 0;
    int pixelIndex = 0;
```

```
for (int y = 0; y < _writeableBitmap.PixelHeight; y++)
{
    for (int x = 0; x < _writeableBitmap.PixelWidth; x++)
    {
        // for each pixel x, y, get the perlin noise value
        // between 0 and 1.
        float normalizedPixel =
                _perlinNoiseImpl.GetMultiscalePerlinNoise(x, y, z);

        // use the value between 0 and 1 to obtain the color value
        // from the color map
        _writeableBitmap.Pixels[pixelIndex] =
                    _colorMap.GetIntColor(normalizedPixel);

        pixelIndex++;
    }
}

// refresh image
_writeableBitmap.Invalidate();
}
```

From Perlin noise, we obtain a number between 0 and 1 and then we use `_colorMap` to get a blended color based on the number.

For optimal results, please make sure the `ImageProcessing` and `PerlinNoise` libraries are compiled with the optimization flag on, and run the application outside of a VS 2010 debugger.

The following is a static image of the clouds:

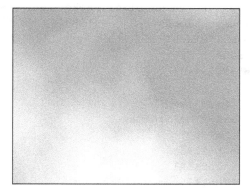

Fire simulation

Here we want to simulate a bonfire rising up from the ground. This differs from simulating clouds in the following respects:

- Fire has a shape with the highest flame concentrated near the center while the sides of the fire are usually lower.

- Fire has colors changing from bright yellowish to orange, to red from the bottom to the top.

- The fire pattern is different from the clouds in terms of its texture. Perlin called noise producing fire texture – **turbulence flow**. The Multi-scale Perlin noise algorithm for calculating turbulence flow is different in the sense that it sums up the absolute values of basic Perlin noise at different octaves (see http://www.noisemachine.com/talk1/22.html).

The fire simulation code is located under project `PerlinFire` within the `PerlinFire.sln` solution. Just like the cloud project, it refers to `PerlinNoise` and `ImageProcessing` projects.

Here is the XAML code for the `PerlinFire` project:

```
<UserControl
    x:Class="PerlinFire.MainPage"
    xmlns="http://schemas.microsoft.com/winfx/2006/xaml/presentation"
    xmlns:x="http://schemas.microsoft.com/winfx/2006/xaml"
    xmlns:d="http://schemas.microsoft.com/expression/blend/2008"
    xmlns:mc="http://schemas.openxmlformats.org/markup-
compatibility/2006"
    mc:Ignorable="d">

    <!-- Grid panel, providing black background -->
    <Grid x:Name="LayoutRoot"
          Background="Black"
          Width="500"
          Height="300">

        <!-- fire image -->
        <Image x:Name="TheFireImage"
               Width="300"
               Height="300"
               HorizontalAlignment="Center"
               VerticalAlignment="Bottom" />
    </Grid>
</UserControl>
```

It is as simple as the XAML code for cloud simulation. The grid panel provides the black background, while the image shows the fire itself.

Most of the interesting code is located within the `MainPage.xaml.cs` code-behind file.

Just like in the case of the Perlin cloud generator, the `MainPage` constructor sets the noise attributes. As you can see, it also sets the `PostProcessingFunction` parameter for the noise. This function will take an absolute value of basic Perlin noise at different octaves before summing it up to obtain multi-scale Perlin noise:

```
public MainPage()
{
    InitializeComponent();

    // perlin noise generator
    _perlinNoiseImpl = new PerlinNoiseImpl();

    // set perlin noise parameters
    _perlinNoiseImpl.Amplitude = 0.6f;
    _perlinNoiseImpl.NumberOctaves = 5;
    _perlinNoiseImpl.XFrequency = 0.013f;
    _perlinNoiseImpl.YFrequency = 0.013f;
    _perlinNoiseImpl.ZFrequency = 0.013f;
    _perlinNoiseImpl.Persistence = 0.8f;

    // set the post processing function to Math.Abs
    // since that will produce the turbulent flow.
    _perlinNoiseImpl.PostProcessingFunction = (f) => Math.Abs(f);

    TheFireImage.Loaded += MainPage_Loaded;
}
```

A lot on initialization is done within the `MainPage_Loaded` method:

```
void MainPage_Loaded(object sender, RoutedEventArgs e)
{
    // for performance sake make the image
    // with 1 image pixels per 16 Silverlight pixels.
    _width = (int)TheFireImage.Width / 4;
    _height = (int)TheFireImage.Height / 4;

    // create the writeable map
    _writeableBitmap =
        new WriteableBitmap
```

```
        (
            _width,
            _height
        );

    // create the array for containing the static image
    _gradientImage = new DoubleColor[_width * _height];

    TheFireImage.Source = _writeableBitmap;
    Color color1 = Color.FromArgb(0x00, 0x00, 0x00, 0x00); //
transparent
    Color color2 = Color.FromArgb(0xFF, 0xC5, 0x01, 0x06); // red
    Color color3 = Color.FromArgb(0xFF, 0xF5, 0xF1, 0x00); // yellow
    Color color4 = Color.FromArgb(0xFF, 0xFF, 0xF6, 0xF7); // whitish

    // set the color map for the static image
    _gradientColorMap = new ColorMap(_height);
    _gradientColorMap.AddChunkWithNormalizedOffset(color1, 0);
    _gradientColorMap.AddChunkWithNormalizedOffset(color2, 0.5);
    _gradientColorMap.AddChunkWithNormalizedOffset(color3, 0.9);
    _gradientColorMap.AddChunkWithNormalizedOffset(color4, 1);

    // set the color map for the dynamically changing part
    _noiseColorMap = new ColorMap(_height);
    _noiseColorMap.AddChunkWithNormalizedOffset(color3, 0);
    _noiseColorMap.AddChunkWithNormalizedOffset(color2, 0.3);
    _noiseColorMap.AddChunkWithNormalizedOffset(color1, 1);

    int bitmapIdx = 0;

    // set the static _gradientImage and _writeableMap
    // to contain the static image
    for (int y = 0; y < _height; y++)
    {
        for (int x = 0; x < _width; x++)
        {
            float normalizedY = ((float)y) / ((float)_height);
            _gradientImage[bitmapIdx] =
                (DoubleColor)_gradientColorMap.GetColor(normalizedY);

            _writeableBitmap.Pixels[bitmapIdx] =
                _gradientColorMap.GetIntColor(normalizedY);

            bitmapIdx++;
```

```
        }
    }

    _writeableBitmap.Invalidate();

    CompositionTarget.Rendering += CompositionTarget_Rendering;
}
```

The method that refreshes the image and produces the fire simulation effect is
CompositionTarget_Rendering. It changes the noise parameters to imitate the fire
movements, calculates the multi-scale Perlin noise, blends it with the background
gradient image, and shapes it to converge at the top:

```
void CompositionTarget_Rendering(object sender, EventArgs e)
{
    // set offsets - make the fire move up and change
    for (int octaveIdx = 0;
            octaveIdx < _perlinNoiseImpl.NumberOctaves;
            octaveIdx++)
    {
        // move the fire up Y axis
        _perlinNoiseImpl.OctaveOffsets[octaveIdx].YOffset += 1f;

        // Changes fire creating turbulence
        _perlinNoiseImpl.OctaveOffsets[octaveIdx].ZOffset += 0.5f;
    }

    int bitmapIdx = 0;

    int midPointX = _width / 2;

    for (int y = 0; y < _height; y++)
    {
        for (int x = 0; x < _width; x++)
        {
            // get the normalized Perlin noise pixel
            // between 0 and 1.
            float normalizedPixel =
                _perlinNoiseImpl.GetMultiscalePerlinNoise(x, y, 0);

            // blends the top of the fire into the background
            // (remember that y = 0 corresponds to the top
            // of the fire picture because of the way the
            // Silverlight coordinates are).
            float factorY = ((float)y) / ((float)_height);
```

```
// distance from the middle point of the fire
// along axis X
int distanceFromMidPointX = Math.Abs(midPointX - x);

// factorX is 0 at the sides of the fire, 1 at
// the mid point of
// the fire along X axis and changes linearly from the
// sides to the mid point. It helps the fire to get a
"cone"
// shape with the middle being "taller" than the sides.
float factorX =
If - (float)distanceFromMidPointX / (float)midPointX;

float totalFactor = factorY * factorX;

// we blend static image located in _gradientImage
// and dynamic image obtained from _noiseColorMap
// and multiply the result by the total factor
_writeableBitmap.Pixels[bitmapIdx] =
    (_gradientImage[bitmapIdx].
        Blend((DoubleColor)_noiseColorMap.
            GetColor(normalizedPixel), 0.4f)).
    Times(totalFactor).ToInt();
bitmapIdx++;
        }
    }

    // refreshes the image
    _writeableBitmap.Invalidate();
}
```

These methods are well documented and you should read the comments in the code. The following, however, is a short but important overview of what is going on within the code:

- Using _gradientColorMap, we can create a static image of fire gradients changing from the bottom to the top:

- Using Perlin noise and `_noiseColorMap`, we can create a dynamic turbulent image of moving fire. The following is how it looks at some instance without the static image:

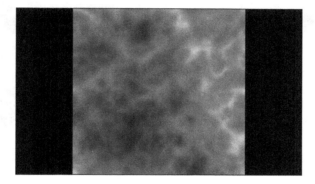

- When we blend these two images with blend factor 0.4, the following is what we get:

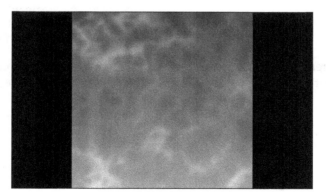

- Finally we use scaling factors – `factorY` to blend the top of the fire into the black background and `factorX` to reduce the fire on the sides changing its shape from rectangular to cone-like. The following is what we get after applying it:

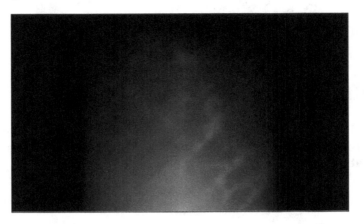

Reminder

For optimal results, please compile the `PerlinNoise` and `ImageProcessing` libraries with the optimization flag on, and run the application outside of the studio's debugger. Enjoy!

Summary

In this chapter, we introduced Perlin noise – which is currently the most popular algorithm for simulating random textures and processes. We gave detailed explanations for basic Perlin noise and multi-scale Perlin noise calculations, and presented implementation of the Perlin noise algorithms in Silverlight. Finally, we provided code and explanations for Perlin noise cloud and fire simulations.

In the next chapter we will talk about three-dimensional animation capabilities in Silverlight starting with projection transform and ending with the description of the XNA subset available in Silverlight.

4
3D Animations in Silverlight

Silverlight provides perspective transform for creating simple 3D effects. Silverlight also allows using part of the XNA framework functionality with support for 3D models, effects, and creating vertex and pixel shaders, giving the developers a lot of power. Both these methods are described in this chapter.

Perspective transform

Perspective transform (also sometimes called **projection transform**) enables the developers to position or move Silverlight (2D) objects within 3D space. It is invaluable for creating simple but effective 3D animations, for example, for Silverlight banners.

Let's explain perspective transform while describing the corresponding sample located under the SAMPLES\CODE\ProjectionSample folder. This sample allows you to investigate all of the parameters of the perspective transform.

Perspective transform in Silverlight is achieved by setting the Projection property of a Silverlight object to contain the PlaneProjection object, whose parameters define the parameters of perspective transform. These parameters include three rotation angles corresponding to rotation around each axis X, Y, and Z, 3D coordinates of the center of rotation, global offset, specifying 3D translation in the viewer's coordinates and local offset, specifying the 3D translation in the coordinates that rotate together with the object.

All the properties of the PlaneProjection object are dependency properties and can be animated using Silverlight animations and storyboards.

Our sample demonstrates what happens when any of the parameters of the
`PlaneProjection` object changes. Here is what you get when you run it and
move some `Slider` controls:

The sliders are connected (via Silverlight bindings) to different properties of
the `PlaneProjection` transform applied to a `Grid` object containing some text.
As a result, the `Grid` object moves in 3D space.

All of the relevant code is located in the `MainPage.xaml` file. The following is the part
of the code that defines a `Grid` panel with text and its `PlaneProjection` transform:

```
<!-- bluish grid with text that is changed by
        the Projection transform -->
<Grid x:Name="TheRotatingGrid"
        Width="500"
        Height="250"
        Background="AliceBlue">

    <!-- Some text to spice up the otherwise
            empty Grid Panel-->
```

```
<TextBlock HorizontalAlignment="Center"
           VerticalAlignment="Top"
           FontSize="30"
           Text="This is the rotating panel" />
<!-- projection transform -->
<Grid.Projection>
    <PlaneProjection x:Name="ThePlaneProjection" />
</Grid.Projection>
</Grid>
```

Under the `Grid` object, there are the `Slider` controls for changing different properties of the `Grid` object's `PlaneProjection` transform. Here is how the `Slider` control's `Value` property connects to `RotationX` of the `PlaneProjection` transform:

```
<Slider Minimum="0"
        Maximum="360"
        Name="RotationX"
        Value="{Binding Path=Projection.RotationX,
                    ElementName=TheRotatingGrid,
                    Mode=TwoWay}" />
```

Overall the `PlaneProjection` transform has 12 properties:

- `RotationX`, `RotationY`, and `RotationZ` control rotations along the *X*, *Y*, and *Z* axes correspondingly

- `CenterOfRotationX`, `CenterOfRotationY`, and `CenterOfRotationZ` control the location of the center of rotation

- `GlobalOffsetX`, `GlobalOffsetY`, and `GlobalOffsetZ` shift the location of the transformed element along the *X*, *Y*, and *Z* axes of the viewer (their orientation won't change with rotation)

- `LocalOffsetX`, `LocalOffsetY`, and `LocalOffsetZ` shift the location of the transformed element along the *X*, *Y*, and *Z* axes of the transformed element – in the beginning local axes are the same as the global ones, but the local axes rotate in 3D space together with the element

Perspective transform is fully integrated into Silverlight and will perform on multiple platforms (it will run on Mac), but can be used only for creating simple 3D objects and animation. Complex 3D models with lighting require Silverlight 5 three-dimensional functionality described in the next section.

Silverlight 5 three-dimensional functionality

Silverlight 5 introduced real 3D capabilities via access to a simplified version of XNA. Using this functionality one can build real complex 3D models of triangles, and create vertex and pixel shaders utilizing the full power of GPU to display them.

There are some shortcomings, however, to the new functionality provided. They are as follows:

- It is not multiplatform – it will only run on Windows (though it is multi-browser).

- If run within a browser, the client will be required to allow the *blocked display drivers* for that website and this might be a nuisance if you want your 3D animations to be widely available.

- The 3D code is essentially not part of the Silverlight framework. It is standalone functionality and the developer needs to spend some extra time and effort in order to make it interact properly with the rest of the Silverlight application.

3D models

3D models usually consist of triangles of different sizes. If the model looks smooth, this means that its triangles are small enough for the user not to notice the singularities.

The vertices of all the triangles that belong to a model are called the **model vertices**.

Vertex and pixel shaders

Vertex and pixel shaders are snippets of code that execute in a highly parallelized fashion on the **GPU** (**Graphics Processing Unit**). They are required to display 3D Silverlight models (unless you use some pre-built shaders as part of the built-in 3D effects).

Vertex shader functionality takes the vertices of the model from the application and transforms them into the pixel's shader input data. It is executed in parallel for each vertex within the model.

The pixel shader actually creates and displays the pixels based on the information obtained from the vertex shader. Pixel shaders are usually executed in parallel for all the pixels.

The following diagram shows interaction between the C# application, the vertex shaders, and the pixel shaders:

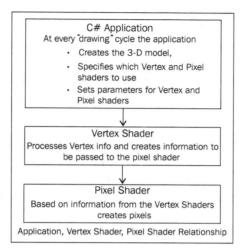

Application, Vertex Shader, Pixel Shader Relationship

The shaders are written in **HLSL (High Level Shader Language)** and are located in separate files. We are not going to describe the HLSL in detail, providing instead some insights into its basic functionality that will allow the reader to build some 3D applications and to acquire some foundation for a deeper study. For those who want to study HLSL at a higher level, I recommend, for example, `http://tinyurl.com/crash-course-in-hlsl`.

Vertex shader source code is usually placed in files with the extension `.hlsl.vs`, while pixel shader source code is placed in files with the extension `.hlsl.ps`.

Compiling pixel shaders

In order to be able to compile the shaders, you need to download and install DirectX SDK from `http://www.microsoft.com/en-us/download/details.aspx?id=6812`.

At the installation path you'll find the shader compiler `fxc`. On a 32-bit Windows system it should be located under `C:\Program Files\Microsoft DirectX SDK (June 2010)\Utilities\bin\x86` folder, while on a 64-bit system it is located under `C:\Program Files (x86)\Microsoft DirectX SDK (June 2010)\Utilities\bin\x86`. In order to make the `fxc` shader compiler available to any application, add the path containing the compiler to the System `PATH` variable by going through the following steps:

1. Open **Control Panel | System**.
2. Click on **Advanced system settings** on the left-hand side of the window.

3. Click on the **Environment Variables** button on the opened panel.

4. Choose the **Path** variable from among the system variables.

5. Click on the **Edit** button at the bottom.

6. Add a separation semicolon **;** followed by the path to the compiler to a **Variable** value.

7. Click on the **OK** button on the **Edit System Variable** window.

8. Again click on the **OK** button on the **Environment Variables** window.

Vertex and pixel shader source code is compiled into `.vs` and `.ps` binary files , respectively, which can be used by the C# application. The shader compilation can be configured to happen when the application runs, but it will consume a lot of CPU resources and slow down the initialization state. It is better to compile the shader code when during the C# application compilation, and add the resulting binary files as application resources.

Enabling your Visual Studio 2010 SP1 or Visual Studio 2012 to create and compile shaders

The shader compiler `fxc` can be used from the command line. After the shader compilation, the binary files can be added to the application as the resources and the whole application can be re-built. This method of compilation, however, requires switching between the command line and the studio every time a shader changes, making the development less productive. In my experience, it is worthwhile to go through a bit of extra pain once and then use the studio to create, modify, and compile the shaders.

Adding shader compilation to your Visual Studio 2010 SP1 project

The following is what you should do in order to be able to compile the shaders from within VS 2010 SP1:

- Download and install Visual Studio 2010 SP1 SDK from
  `http://www.microsoft.com/en-us/download/details.aspx?id=21835`

- Download and install HLSL Shader Build Task from
  `http://code.msdn.microsoft.com/HLSL-Shader-Build-Task-285e9b53`

The previous steps will allow you to compile the shader files once you add these to a project and set their `Build Action` property to `VertexShader` or `PixelShader`. In order for the VS 2010 to be able to assign `VertexShader` and `PixelShader` build actions, you need to add the following code to the corresponding project file:

```
<ItemGroup Condition="'$(BuildingInsideVisualStudio)'=='true'">
  <AvailableItemName Include="VertexShader">
    <Visible>false</Visible>
  </AvailableItemName>
  <AvailableItemName Include="PixelShader">
    <Visible>false</Visible>
  </AvailableItemName>
</ItemGroup>
<UsingTask TaskName="ShaderBuildTask.ShaderCompile"
           AssemblyName="ShaderBuildTask, Version=1.0.3072.18169,
Culture=neutral, PublicKeyToken=44e467d1687af125" />
<Target Name="VertexShaderCompile"
        Condition="'@(VertexShader)' != '' "
        BeforeTargets="BeforeBuild">
  <ShaderCompile Sources="@(VertexShader)"
                 ShaderProfile="vs_2_0"
                 IntermediateOutputPath="$(IntermediateOutputPath)">
    <Output TaskParameter="Outputs" ItemName="Resource" />
  </ShaderCompile>
</Target>
<Target Name="PixelShaderCompile"
        Condition="'@(PixelShader)' != '' "
        BeforeTargets="BeforeBuild">
  <ShaderCompile Sources="@(PixelShader)"
                 ShaderProfile="ps_2_0"
                 IntermediateOutputPath="$(IntermediateOutputPath)">
    <Output TaskParameter="Outputs"
            ItemName="Resource" />
  </ShaderCompile>
</Target>
```

The code can be added right above the following lines:

```
<!-- This property group is only here to support building this
project using the
      MSBuild 3.5 toolset. In order to work correctly with this older
toolset, it needs
      to set the TargetFrameworkVersion to v3.5 -->
<PropertyGroup Condition="'$(MSBuildToolsVersion)' == '3.5'">
```

Once you add this code to the .csproj file after reloading the project, you will see VertexShader and PixelShader build action options for any file within that project.

Now, to create a shader within a project whose project file was modified as previously described, you need to go through the following steps:

1. Create a new file under the project using a **Text File** template for it.

2. Rename the file to have a proper name and extension (for a vertex shader file the extension should be `vs.hlsl` while for a pixel shader file, the extension is `ps.hlsl`).

3. Visual Studio 2010 creates the new file as a Unicode file. Unfortunately, the `fxc` compiler breaks on the Unicode files. We need to change the file encoding. To do this within the studio perform the following steps:

    i. Open the file, for example, by double-clicking on it within the **Solution Explorer** window. Then go to the **File** menu and choose the **Save** `<filename>` **As** option. Do not change the name of the file. Instead go to the **Save** button at the bottom of the window and press on the arrow on the right-hand side of it:

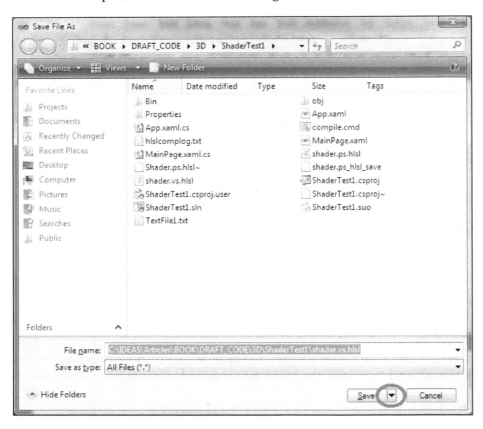

ii. Choose the **Save with Encoding ...** option.

iii. Choose **US-ASCII** in the encoding dialog.

iv. Press **OK**.

Finally, the shader file is ready to be written into and compiled.

Adding shader compilation to your Visual Studio 2012 project

Shader compilation under VS 2012 is different from shader compilation under VS 2010. In some respects it is easier – you do not have to download and install anything to run a shader compilation (everything that's needed comes together with the VS 2012). In other respects it is a bit more difficult – there has not yet been created anything similar to HLSL Shader Build Task for Silverlight and for every shader file we are forced to add the compiled shader files as a resource to the VS 2012 project. In VS 2012, the `fxc` compiler comes together with the studio, so you do not have to add DirectX SDK. The compiler is located under `C:\Program Files\Windows Kits\8.0\bin\x86` for 32-bit machines and in `C:\Program Files\Windows Kits\8.0\bin\x64` for 64-bit machines.

Please add the folder containing the `fxc` compiler to the `PATH` variable as was described in the previous subsection.

VS 2012 also contains an MS build task for building the shader files. Unfortunately, this task is only available for C++ projects and is not available for Silverlight ones.

The following are the points to keep in mind in order to ensure that your VS 2012 project builds the shader files and adds the results as resources to the project:

- Make sure that the `fxc` compiler is in the `PATH` variable by adding the corresponding folder to the `PATH` variable.

- VS 2012 should be re-started after the `fxc` folder is added to the `PATH`.

- Create the vertex and pixel shader files (in our case their names are `shader.vs.hlsl` and `shader.ps.hlsl` respectively) within the project just like you would for VS 2010. Set their `Build Action` property to `None`.

- Change the encoding for the `shader.vs.hlsl` and `shader.ps.hlsl` files in exactly the same way as was described for VS 2010.

- Add new items `shader.vs` and `shader.ps` to the project. For example, you can create them as text files.

- Change their `Build Action` property to `Resource`.

- Right-click on the project name within **Solution Explorer** and choose **Properties**. Within the opened **Properties** panel, choose the **Build Events** option on the left-hand side. Add the following two lines to the **Pre-build event command line** editable area:

```
fxc /nologo /E"main" /T vs_2_0 /Fo "$(ProjectDir)shader.vs" /Od
/Zi $(ProjectDir)SHADER.VS.HLSL
```

```
fxc /nologo /E"main" /T ps_2_0 /Fo "$(ProjectDir)shader.ps" /Od
/Zi $(ProjectDir)SHADER.PS.HLSL
```

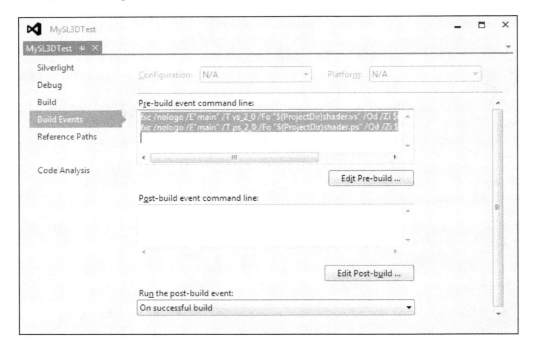

Now if you put the correct shader code in the `shader.vs.hlsl` and `shader.ps.hlsl` files, and then build the project, the empty `shader.vs` and `shader.ps` files will be overridden with the compiled shader code and added to the resulting `.dll` file as resources.

Also note that (unlike VS 2010), VS 2012 provides syntax highlighting for shader file content.

Creating the moving triangle application

Here we show how to build triangle 3D animation. The code for this sample is located under the SAMPLES\CODE\MovingTriangle folder.

Try running this sample! During the first run, most likely you'll get the following warning message: **Please enable your graphics drivers and reload the application**. In order to be able to run the 3D application, you need to do the following:

1. Right mouse click onto this warning message (or anywhere around it).
2. Click on **Silverlight**.
3. Choose the **Permissions** tab, find and select the URL corresponding to the application (usually if you view it on the same machine, you'll be able to tell the correct URL by the port number).

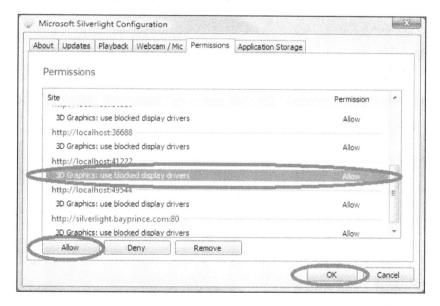

4. Click on the **Allow** button at the bottom of the dialog box.
5. Click on the **OK** button.
6. Now restart the application if you are running it in the debugger, or restart the browser to refresh the application if you are running the application on a website.

When you run the application successfully, you will see a tricolored triangle rotating in 3D around the *Y*-axis:

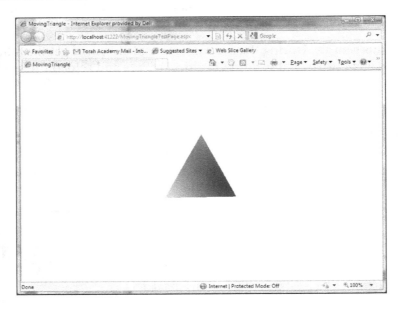

Now, let's look at the code.

First, to use the 3D functionality we need to enable GPU acceleration, by modifying the `MovingTriangleTestPage.aspx` file to contain the following parameter setting under its `silverlightControlHost` tag:

```
<param name="EnableGPUAcceleration" value="true" />
```

We also need to add a bunch of `.dll` references to Silverlight .NET DLLs containing `.Xna` in its name. Here is the list of the DLLs you should add:

- **Microsoft.Xna.Framework**
- **Microsoft.Xna.Framework.Graphics**
- **Microsoft.Xna.Framework.Graphics.Extensions**
- **Microsoft.Xna.Framework.Graphics.Shaders**
- **Microsoft.Xna.Framework.Math**
- **System.Windows.Xna**

All the 3D processing takes place within a Silverlight control called `DrawingSurface`, and all of it takes place within the C# files (not in XAML), so that the only thing we need to add to XAML for 3D display is the `DrawingSurface` tag. The following is how our `MainPage.xaml` file looks:

```xml
<UserControl x:Class="MovingTriangle.MainPage"
    xmlns="http://schemas.microsoft.com/winfx/2006/xaml/presentation"
    xmlns:x="http://schemas.microsoft.com/winfx/2006/xaml"
    xmlns:d="http://schemas.microsoft.com/expression/blend/2008"
    xmlns:mc="http://schemas.openxmlformats.org/markup-
compatibility/2006"
    mc:Ignorable="d">

    <Grid x:Name="LayoutRoot" Background="White">
        <!-- DrawingSurface control can host
            3-D models -->
        <DrawingSurface x:Name="TheDrawingSurface" />

        <!-- the warning text to be shown
            in case the client did not set permissions
            to run 3-D applications from this URL -->
        <TextBlock
            x:Name="GraphicsDriversNeedToBeEnabledText"
            Text="Please enable your graphics drivers and reload the
application"
            FontSize="20"
            Visibility="Collapsed"
            HorizontalAlignment="Center"
            VerticalAlignment="Center"/>
    </Grid>
</UserControl>
```

Aside from the `DrawingSurface` XML tag, all the code dealing with 3D is located either within the `MainPage.xaml.cs` file or within the shaders.

The C# code is also quite simple. As you can see there are two important functions dealing with 3D – `Initial3DSetup` and `TheDrawingSurface_Draw`. The `Initial3DSetup` function takes care of things that need to be done only once during the application run:

- It creates the model:
  ```csharp
  // create some XNA colors for the vertices
  Color red = new Color(255, 0, 0, 255);
  Color blue = new Color(0, 0, 255, 255);
  Color green = new Color(0, 255, 0, 255);

  // create the positions for triangle's vertices as
  // 2-D vectors
  Vector3 top = new Vector3(0, 2, 0);
  Vector3 bottomLeft = new Vector3(-1, -1, 0);
  ```

```
Vector3 bottomRight = new Vector3(1, -1, 0);

// create an array of vertices to be passed to the
// vertex buffer. Adding different
// colors to each of the vertices
VertexPositionColor[] vertices =
    new VertexPositionColor[]
{
    new VertexPositionColor(top, red),
    new VertexPositionColor(bottomRight, green),
    new VertexPositionColor(bottomLeft, blue),
};
```

- It sets the vertex buffer:

```
// create the vertex buffer of length 3
_vertexBuffer =
    new VertexBuffer
    (
        _graphicsDevice,
        VertexPositionColor.VertexDeclaration,
        vertices.Length,
        BufferUsage.WriteOnly
    );

// set the vertex buffer to contain the array of the vertices
_vertexBuffer.SetData(0, vertices, 0, vertices.Length, 0);
```

- It gets the compiled shader code from the application resources into
  the _vertexShader and _pixelShader class fields:

```
// pull the vertex shader code out of the resource file shader.vs
created
// at the compilation state from shader.hlsl.vs source code file
// and set the _vertexShader variable to contain it
using (Stream vertexShaderStream =
    Application.GetResourceStream
    (
        new Uri
        (
            @"MovingTriangle;component/shader.vs",
            UriKind.Relative
        )).Stream)
{
    _vertexShader =
        VertexShader.FromStream(_graphicsDevice,
```

```
vertexShaderStream);
}

// pull the pixel shader code out of the resource file shader.ps
created
// at the compilation state from shader.hlsl.ps source code file
// and set the _vertexShader variable to contain it
using (Stream pixelShaderStream =
    Application.GetResourceStream
    (
        new Uri
        (
            @"MovingTriangle;component/shader.ps",
            UriKind.Relative
        )).Stream)
{
    _pixelShader =
        PixelShader.FromStream(_graphicsDevice,
pixelShaderStream);
}
```

The function `TheDrawingSurface_Draw` is set to be the event handler for the `TheDrawingSurface.Draw` event, fired to redraw the 3D model within the `DrawingSurface` control.

Here, we do not have space to explain the 3D processing in much detail. However, before we dive into the `TheDrawingSurface_Draw` function, it is good to provide some basics on what is going on.

In 3D processing, the transform applied to the models is usually split into the following three parts:

- **Model transform**: This corresponds to the rotations and translations of the 3D model itself
- **Camera** (or **view**) **transform**: This describes the position of the camera
- **Projection transform**: This describes how the 3D model maps into the 2D image

The total transform is the product of all these three transforms. In our case, to rotate the image, we change the model transform as time progresses, and keep camera and projection transforms the same.

The following is the body of the `TheDrawingSurface_Draw` function with comments:

```
// prevents the back side of the shape from being "culled"
// otherwise the back side of the triangle won't be seen
_graphicsDevice.RasterizerState = new RasterizerState
    {
        CullMode = CullMode.None
    };

_graphicsDevice.Clear // clear the image buffer
(
    ClearOptions.DepthBuffer | ClearOptions.Target,
    new Color(0, 0, 0, 0),
    10f,
    0
);

// set the vertex buffer of the graphics device
// to contain our _vertexBuffer class variable
_graphicsDevice.SetVertexBuffer(_vertexBuffer);
_graphicsDevice.SetVertexShader(_vertexShader);// set the vertex
shader
_graphicsDevice.SetPixelShader(_pixelShader);// set the pixel shader

// make the rotation angle dependent on total time passes
// in order to rotate the model
float rotationAngle =
    (float) (MathHelper.PiOver4 * e.TotalTime.TotalSeconds);
// create the model transform

// rotate the model by changing the model's transform
Matrix modelTransform =
    Matrix.CreateRotationY(rotationAngle);

// set the camera view to be 10 units away from the model on Z axis.
Matrix viewTransform =
    Matrix.CreateLookAt(new Vector3(0, 0, 5), Vector3.Zero, Vector3.
Up);

// set the properties of projection transform that maps 3-D view
// into 2-D image (in fact we are setting the view frustum properties)
Matrix projectionTransform =
    Matrix.CreatePerspectiveFieldOfView
        (
            MathHelper.PiOver2, // field view is 90 degrees
```

```
        1, // aspect ratio
        1, // near plane 1 unit away
        10 // far plane is 10 units away
    );


// result transform is the product of all three transforms above
Matrix resultTransform =
    modelTransform *
    viewTransform *
    projectionTransform;


// set the vertex shader's 1st parameter to be the transform matrix
_graphicsDevice.SetVertexShaderConstantFloat4(0, ref resultTransform);


_graphicsDevice.DrawPrimitives// force the redrawing of the
SurfaceControl
(
    PrimitiveType.TriangleList,
    0,
    _vertexBuffer.VertexCount/3
);


e.InvalidateSurface();// force the "Draw" event to be called again
```

For this example, the simplest shaders are used. The following is the
VertexShader code:

```
// transformation matrix provided by the application
float4x4 totalTransformMatrix;

// vertex data structure that
// is input to the vertex shader
struct VertexData
{
  float3 Position : POSITION;
  float4 Color : COLOR;
};

// data structure containing
// the output from the vertex shader
struct VertexShaderOutput
{
  float4 Position : POSITION;
  float4 Color : COLOR;
};
```

```
// main shader function
VertexShaderOutput main(VertexData vertex)
{
  VertexShaderOutput output;

  // apply the transformation to
  // the vertex position.
  output.Position = mul(float4(vertex.Position,1),
totalTransformMatrix);

  // pass the color through to the next stage
  output.Color = vertex.Color;
  return output;
}
```

And the following is the PixelShader code:

```
// output from the vertex shader serves as input
// to the pixel shader
struct VertexShaderOutput
{
  float4 Position : POSITION;
  float4 Color : COLOR;
};

// main shader function
float4 main(VertexShaderOutput vertex) : COLOR
{
  return vertex.Color;
}
```

The moving prism application

We can spice up the model a little bit by creating a rotating prism, instead of the rotating triangle. The MovingPrismApplication project is located under the SAMPLES\CODE\ MovingPrismApplication folder.

When running MovingPrismApplication, do not forget to set the driver permissions for that application, just as you did for MovingTriangle.

The following is a screenshot of the moving prism:

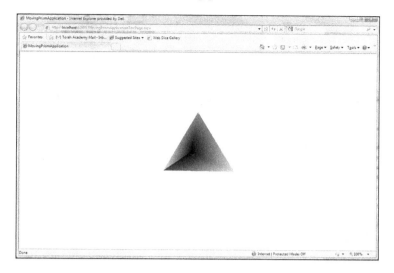

The only differences from the `MovingTriangle` project are the following:

- The fourth vertex is being created shifted along the Z-axis from the rest of the vertices:

```
// the 4th vertext to create the prism
Vector3 zVertex = new Vector3(0, 0, 1);
```

- The `vertices` array contains 12 vertices instead of 3; each three consecutive vertices corresponding to a side of the prism:

```
// create an array of vertices
// corresponding to the triangles
// corresponding to the sides of the prism.
// the same vertices will be repeated
// for different sides if needed
VertexPositionColor[] vertices =
    new VertexPositionColor[]
{
    new VertexPositionColor(top, red),
    new VertexPositionColor(bottomRight, green),
    new VertexPositionColor(bottomLeft, blue),
    new VertexPositionColor(top, red),
    new VertexPositionColor(bottomRight, green),
    new VertexPositionColor(zVertex, black),
    new VertexPositionColor(bottomLeft, green),
    new VertexPositionColor(top, red),
```

```
        new VertexPositionColor(zVertex, black),
        new VertexPositionColor(bottomRight, green),
        new VertexPositionColor(bottomLeft, blue),
        new VertexPositionColor(zVertex, black),
};
```

The 3D related topics that were left out

There is much more that can be said about 3D processing, but unfortunately due to time and space constraints, I'll have to leave it out for now. The following is a list of some other 3D topics that should be learned by those who want to have a good mastery of the subject:

- By using shaders that are more complex, you can create numerous 3D effects, including lighting, moving objects along some trajectories, and many others. I would recommend studying the HLSL and 3D math in order to be able to do that.

- Most developers prefer to create effects absorbing the complexity of interacting with specific vertex and pixel shaders. The purpose of the effect object is to pass parameters to the shaders and invoke the shaders when needed. Creating custom effects deserves a topic of its own.

- There is a bunch of built-in effects available from Silverlight XNA libraries. Studying these effects can also be of great help.

- Usually the complex 3D models are not created in code, but built by external tools and imported into Silverlight. Importing such a model is another topic for suggested study.

Summary

In this chapter, we have discussed different ways of creating 3D animations in Silverlight – using projection transform and using the Silverlight 3D XNA functionality.

The next chapter will provide examples of creating animated banners using Silverlight.

5
Building an Animated Banner

In this chapter, we will apply what we learned to build an animated banner. We will provide a detailed description of the code for creating a text in 3D space and rotating it in order to create a cool animation effect. We will also show how to embed a Silverlight banner into an HTML page .

What we aim to build

The following is a screenshot of the animated banner we will attempt to build in this chapter:

This is a banner from my website awebpros.com. Note that the text appears to wrap around the globe in three dimensions. Moreover, if you run the demo (or visit my website) you will see that after the page is loaded, lines of the text blink and rotate around the globe also in three dimensions. In the rest of the chapter we will describe how this was achieved.

The globe image

The globe image is downloaded from the Microsoft ClipArt website:
http://tinyurl.com/msofficeglobe.

Perspective transform

We will use perspective transform, which was described in the previous
chapter, to create the 3D rotation effects. Unlike the XNA functionality,
it is fully multi-platform – running on Mac computers as well, and is
sufficient to create powerful 3D animations.

Code description

The code for the demo is located under the AnimatedBanner project.

Referring to the globe image within an XAML file

As was previously mentioned, I downloaded the globe image from the Microsoft
ClipArt website and added it to the project as a resource.

The following code will show you how to add the image to the MainPage.xaml file:

```
<Image x:Name="image"
       Source="Globe.png"
       HorizontalAlignment="Center"
       VerticalAlignment="Center"
       Margin="0,0,10,0"
       Width="270">
    <Image.Projection>
        <!-- GlobalOffsetZ for a still image
                controls its Z-depth. I had to play
                with this parameter to create an
                illusion of letters going behind
                the Globe during the rotation-->
        <PlaneProjection GlobalOffsetZ="30" />
    </Image.Projection>
</Image>
```

Creating rotating lines of text

The rotating text lines consist of individual `TextBlock` elements corresponding to each letter within them. The `Projection` property of each of the `TextBlock` elements is set to place the corresponding letter at the appropriate location within 3D space.

Horizontal rotation is achieved by changing the `RotationY` parameter of the perspective transform, while the distance from the center of rotation is controlled by the `LocalOffsetZ` parameter.

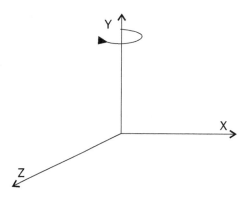

In order to achieve the effect of the text going behind the globe image during the rotation, we can tweak its `LocalOffsetZ` parameter as well as the parameter controlling the Z-Depth of the globe image (since the image is still, it can be either its `GlobalOffsetZ` or `LocalOffsetZ` parameter).

In order for the letters to go behind and in front of the image during the rotation, both `TextBlocks` corresponding to the letters and the image have to belong to the same panel. Because of this, we cannot implement the lines of text arranged in a circular 3D fashion as a separate Silverlight control. Indeed, controls always have their own visual tree so that all of its subcomponents belong to some top-level component, and in that case, the individual letters would belong to some visual component within the text control, and not to the same panel as the image does. Therefore, in order to automate the text creation without creating a special control, we build a class `RotatedTextFactory`. Its purpose is to create `TextBlocks` and add them to a `Panel` control, arranging them around the *Y*-axis in 3D space. It also manages various parameters of the `TextBlocks` and 3D rotations.

There are two attached properties defined within the AttachedProperties static class that manage the 3D position of each *individual* TextBlock corresponding to one letter. The OriginalShift property controls the original position of the letter, while the Shift property controls the position during the animation, that is, in order to rotate a letter we simply change its individual Shift property. (See *Chapter 1, Building Blocks of Animation*, for information about the attached properties). Both OriginalShift and Shift are angular measures in degrees (the same as the RotateY property).

The reason we want to have these two properties instead of simply modifying RotateY is that we use the Shift property to rotate multiple letters at the same time, by the same angle, while OriginalShift is used to arrange the letters sequentially as a text.

You can see that the OriginalShift attached property callback sets the RotationY property to OriginalShift:

```
static void OnOriginalShiftChanged
(
    object sender,
    DependencyPropertyChangedEventArgs e
)
{
    PlaneProjection planeProjection = (PlaneProjection)sender;

    planeProjection.RotationY = (double)e.NewValue;
}
```

And the Shift attached property callback sets the RotationY property to OriginalShift + Shift:

```
static void OnShiftChanged
(
    object sender,
    DependencyPropertyChangedEventArgs e
)
{
    PlaneProjection planeProjection = (PlaneProjection)sender;

    double originalShift = GetOriginalShift(planeProjection);
    double shift = (double)e.NewValue;

    planeProjection.RotationY = originalShift + shift;
}
```

Now back to the `RotatedTextFactory` class, which contains the core functionality of the sample. As was previously mentioned, this class creates the `TextBlock` object for each letter in a line of text, inserts these objects into a `Panel` control, and arranges them to rotate around the Y-axis. The `Panel` control is specified by the `ThePanel` property of the class. It is a dependency property so that we can bind it to the real panel within our XAML file.

The `Text` property of the class holds the line of text to display. The `LocalOffsetZ` property controls the distance from the center of rotation. The function `RecalculateOriginalShifts` sets the `OriginalShift` property of each `TextBlock` element to position them next to one another in order to form the words.

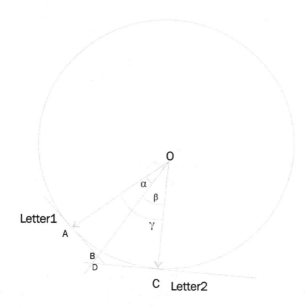

The previous diagram shows how to arrive at a formula for arranging the letters next to one another. It shows the look from above. Point O is the center of rotation. So, |AO| = |CO| = `LocalOffsetZ`. There are two letters shown: the horizontal center of Letter1 is located at point A and the center of Letter2 is located at point C. |AB| is the half width of Letter1 and |CD| is the half width of Letter2. AOB and DOC are right-angled triangles so we see that:

```
tan(α) = |AO|/|AB| = ( (width of Letter1) / 2) / LocalOffsetZ;
```

In a similar fashion, we can derive that:

```
tan(ß) = |AC|/|CD| = ( (width of Letter2) / 2) / LocalOffsetZ
```

So we can see that:

```
γ = α + ß = tan⁻¹(( (width of Letter1) / 2) / LocalOffsetZ) + tan⁻¹( (
(width of Letter2) / 2) / LocalOffsetZ)
```

This is exactly the formula applied to each letter to recalculate the mutual shift between the two adjacent `TextBlock` elements within the function `RecalculateOriginalShifts`. To calculate the `OriginalShift` function's delta for the current letter, it takes half of the width of the previous letter, half of the width of the current letter, applies the formulas above to them by calling the function `HalfAngleFromElementWidth`, and sums up the results.

The property `LocalOffsetY` controls the vertical shift of the line of text (each of our three lines of text have this property set to a different value).

The `TextStyle` property of the `RotatedTextFactory` class gives the user full control over the properties of the `TextBlock` objects via its styles.

Since the `FontSize` parameter is most likely to change from line to line, we also provide a separate a `FontSize` property within the `RotatedTextFactory` class (in order to avoid creating different `Styles` for different lines in case only the `FontSize` property changed).

The `RotatedTextFactory` class not only manages creation of the text line, but also controls its rotation around the *Y*-axis with the help of its `Shift` property. Changing `Shift` on the `RotatedTextFactory` object will rotate the whole line of text by changing the `Shift` attached property on each of the individual `TextBlock` objects within the line of text. `Shift` is a dependency property within the `RotatedTextFactory` class because we want to be able to animate it.

The `RotatedTextFactory` objects are defined as XAML resources of `LayoutRoot` `Grid` within the `MainPage.xaml` file:

```xml
<!--"AWebPros.com" text to rotate-->
<this:RotatedTextFactory x:Key="AWebProsTextFactoryKey"
                    x:Name="AWebProsTextFactory"
                    Text="AWebPros.com"
                    TextStyle="{StaticResource TheTextStyle}"
                    ThePanel="{Binding ElementName=LayoutRoot}"
                    FontSize="35"
                    LocalOffsetY="-50"
                    LocalOffsetZ="125"
```

```
                              StartShift="55" />

<!--"We help people" text to rotate-->
<this:RotatedTextFactory x:Key="WeHelpTextFactoryKey"
                         x:Name="WeHelpTextFactory"
                         Text="We help people"
                         TextStyle="{StaticResource TheTextStyle}"
                         ThePanel="{Binding ElementName=LayoutRoot}"
                         FontSize="30"
                         LocalOffsetY="0"
                         LocalOffsetZ="140"
                         StartShift="40" />

<!--"to deliver!" text to rotate-->
<this:RotatedTextFactory x:Key="ToDeliverTextFactoryKey"
                         x:Name="ToDeliverTextFactory"
                         Text="to deliver!"
                         TextStyle="{StaticResource TheTextStyle}"
                         ThePanel="{Binding ElementName=LayoutRoot}"
                         FontSize="30"
                         LocalOffsetY="50"
                         LocalOffsetZ="120"
                         StartShift="30" />
```

Their properties were tweaked in order to position the lines of text correctly. Once the RotatedTextFactory objects are created and their properties are set, they create the corresponding text and place it within the LayoutRoot panel automatically.

Animation storyboard

The MainPage.xaml file also contains the storyboard to make the top line blink (by changing the opacity of its text) and to make all the lines move around the globe by animating the Shift property of the RotatedTextFactory objects:

```
<Storyboard x:Name="BlinkAndRotateStoryboard"
            FillBehavior="Stop"
            RepeatBehavior="3x">

    <!-- make the top text line blink 3 times by changing its opacity
-->
    <DoubleAnimationUsingKeyFrames
        BeginTime="00:00:00"
        Storyboard.TargetName="AWebProsTextFactory"
        Storyboard.TargetProperty="RotatedTextFactory.TextOpacity"
```

```
                    RepeatBehavior="3x">
        <SplineDoubleKeyFrame KeyTime="00:00:00.2000000"
                                Value="0" />
        <SplineDoubleKeyFrame KeyTime="00:00:00.4000000"
                                Value="1" />
    </DoubleAnimationUsingKeyFrames>

    <!-- Rotate the lines of text one after another-->
    <Storyboard BeginTime="00:00:01.2">
        <!-- rotate the top line -->
        <DoubleAnimation
            Duration="0:0:1"
            By="-360"
            BeginTime="0:0:0"
            Storyboard.TargetProperty="(RotateTextFactory.Shift)"
            Storyboard.TargetName="AWebProsTextFactory" />

        <!-- rotate the middle line -->
        <DoubleAnimation
            Duration="0:0:1"
            By="-360"
            BeginTime="0:0:1"
            Storyboard.TargetProperty="(RotateTextFactory.Shift)"
            Storyboard.TargetName="WeHelpTextFactory" />

        <!-- rotate the bottom line-->
        <DoubleAnimation
            Duration="0:0:1"
            By="-360"
            BeginTime="0:0:2"
            Storyboard.TargetProperty="(RotateTextFactory.Shift)"
            Storyboard.TargetName="ToDeliverTextFactory" />
    </Storyboard>
</Storyboard>
```

We made each of the lines of text rotate consecutively one after another by setting the BeginTime properties of each individual DoubleAnimation to start after the previous line animation is finished.

Now, we want to trigger the storyboard after all the text is loaded and all the letters are arranged around the globe. This can be a little tricky since the function `RecalculateOriginalShifts` that arranges the letters is called multiple times (for example, after each letter becomes visible). Still we call `LettersRearrangedEvent` from within that function. The event handler for this event is set within the `MainPage.xaml.cs` file – it stops the previous instance of the storyboard and starts another instance of it, so that only the last instance of the storyboard has a chance to continue and complete:

```
void RestartStoryboard()
{
    // stop the previous instance of the storyboard run
    _rotateStoryboard.Stop();

    // start a new instance of the storyboard run
    _rotateStoryboard.Begin();
}
```

Placing the Silverlight banner within an HTML file

We want the HTML parameters to control the size of the Silverlight animation. To achieve this, we will place the entire Silverlight `LayoutRoot Grid` inside the Silverlight `Viewbox` control (as you can see in the `MainPage.xaml` file).

Now let's focus our attention on the `AnimatedBanner.Web` project created for us by Visual Studio. This project contains the file `AnimatedBannerTestPage.html`, that provides a sample of embedding our Silverlight control within HTML code.

You can start the browser displaying our Silverlight banner within that HTML page by right-clicking on the file within **Solution Explorer** and choosing **View in Browser**.

Most of this file consists of the code for handling Silverlight errors. This code is not needed once your Silverlight application is debugged.

The following is the part of the code that is actually needed for embedding the Silverlight control into an HTML page:

```
<div id="form1" style="height: 300px; width: 300px">
    <div id="silverlightControlHost">
        <object data="data:application/x-silverlight-2,"
                type="application/x-silverlight-2"
                width="100%" height="100%">
```

```
                <param name="source" value="ClientBin/AnimatedBanner.xap"
    />

                <param name="onError" value="onSilverlightError" />
                <param name="background" value="white" />
                <param name="minRuntimeVersion" value="5.0.61118.0" />
                <param name="autoUpgrade" value="true" />
                <ahref="http://go.microsoft.com/fwlink/?LinkID=149156
    &v=5.0.61118.0"
                    style="text-decoration: none">
                  <img src="http://go.microsoft.com/
    fwlink/?LinkId=161376"
                        alt="Get Microsoft Silverlight"
                        style="border-style: none" />
                </a>
            </object>
        </div>
    </div>
```

The value of the parameter source is pointing to the location of the Silverlight .xap file ClientBin/AnimatedBanner.xap containing the Silverlight application. The hyperlink within the form points to a page to be shown to the client, in case a Silverlight plugin is not installed on the client's machine.

Try changing the height and width parameters within the top line and refreshing the page. You will see that the size of the Silverlight banner is being changed accordingly. This is because we placed the banner within the Silverlight Viewbox control.

By default the Silverlight banner is placed inline, that is, after the previous text. In our case, we have no text on the page so the banner will be located in the top-left corner. We can modify the location by tweaking the HTML parameters – for example setting the parameter float on the top-level div tag to right will move the banner to the top-right corner.

Summary

In this chapter, we applied what we learned in the previous chapters in order to build a cool 3D animated banner and embed it within an HTML page.

A
Creating and starting a Silverlight project

The following steps will aid you in creating and starting a Silverlight project:

1. Open Visual Studio 2010.
2. Choose **File | New | Project** menu item.
3. Choose **Silverlight Application** as a project type, choose the location in which you want to have this project, and choose the project name to be SpinningControlSample.

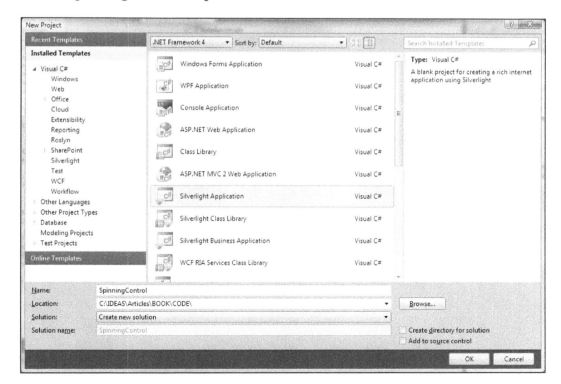

4. Press the **OK** button

5. On the oncoming screen, press the **OK** button again.

You have just created a Silverlight application project. In fact, you can see two projects created – an ASP project hosting the Silverlight application called SpinningControlSample.Web (which we touch only very lightly in this book) and the Silverlight 5 project SpinningControlSample.

One can run the application within Visual Studio debugger, by choosing **Debug | Start Debugging** menu item.

The Silverlight 5 project, SpinningControlSample, is where all the Silverlight work takes place. Building this project produces a Silverlight application deployment file called SpinningControlSample.xap. During the build, this XAP file is copied under the ClientBin folder of the ASP project.

The ASP project SpinningControlSample.web is only used for testing Silverlight applications. It provides ASP and HTML test files SpinningControlSample.aspx and SpinningControlSample.html. One can start the Silverlight application by right-clicking on any of these two files within the **Solution Explorer** window and choosing the **Run in Browser** option.

B
Changing the XAML formatting

This appendix shows how to change the XAML formatting to print each XAML attribute on a separate line. This makes the XAML file more readable and this is the formatting we use in our source code.

1. Open the **Options** window by going to the **Tools** | **Options** menu item.
2. Choose **Text Editor** | **XAML** | **Formatting** | **Spacing** within the left pane.
3. Make sure you have the **Position each attribute on a separate line** and **Position first attribute on same line as start tag** options selected as shown in the following screenshot:

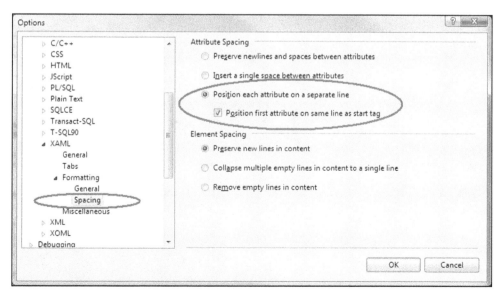

C
Installing snippets

Please follow the following steps to install the Visual Studio 2010 snippets provided with these samples in the Snippets folder:

1. Open Visual Studio 2010.
2. Choose **Tools | Code Snippet Manager** menu item.
3. Once you have the **Code Snippet Manager** window, select the **NetFX30** folder within a folder tree on the left-hand side as shown in the following screenshot:

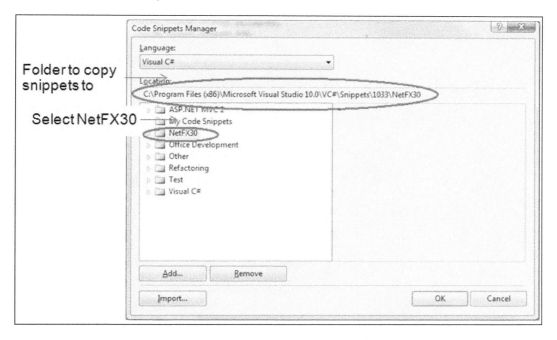

4. Select the location folder at the top of the **Code Snippet Manager** window; right-click on the selection and choose **Copy**.

5. Paste the copied location into a Windows Explorer.

6. Copy all the snippet files from the `Snippet` folder of these sample code into the snippet location on your computer. If a dialog box pops up asking if you really want to override some existing files, click on **Yes**.

D
Using snippets

Here we give an example of snippet usage by showing how to create a dependency property within C# code using propdp snippet. (Creating dependency and attached properties in code would be a pain without snippets).

We are going to create a dependency property RotationAngle of type double within the SpinningControl class.

Within that RotationAngle.cs file, move the cursor to the place you want the dependency property to be at and type propdp<tab>.

The snippet will expand into the following text:

```
#region MyProperty Dependency Property
public int MyProperty
{
    get { return (int)GetValue(MyPropertyProperty); }
    set { SetValue(MyPropertyProperty, value); }
}

public static readonly DependencyProperty MyPropertyProperty =
DependencyProperty.Register
(
    "MyProperty",
    typeof(int),
    typeof(MainPage),
    new PropertyMetadata(0)
);
#endregion MyProperty Dependency Property
```

The changeable strings are selected in orange. Once you change a selectable string, for example, MyProperty to RotationAngle and press *Tab*, the matching strings will change throughout the entire snippet and the next selectable string will be selected. You should change MyProperty to RotationAngle, int to double, and 0 to 0.0. Once you are done, press *Enter* to exit the snippet-editing mode. The following is how the resulting code should look:

```
#region RotationAngle Dependency Property
public double RotationAngle
{
    get { return (double)GetValue(RotationAngleProperty); }
    set { SetValue(RotationAngleProperty, value); }
}

public static readonly DependencyProperty
RotationAngleProperty =
DependencyProperty.Register
(
    "RotationAngle",
    typeof(double),
    typeof(SpinningControl),
    new PropertyMetadata(0.0)
);
#endregion RotationAngle Dependency Property
```

Congratulations! You have just created your first dependency property using propdp snippet.

Index

About Packt Publishing

Packt, pronounced 'packed', published its first book "*Mastering phpMyAdmin for Effective MySQL Management*" in April 2004 and subsequently continued to specialize in publishing highly focused books on specific technologies and solutions.

Our books and publications share the experiences of your fellow IT professionals in adapting and customizing today's systems, applications, and frameworks. Our solution based books give you the knowledge and power to customize the software and technologies you're using to get the job done. Packt books are more specific and less general than the IT books you have seen in the past. Our unique business model allows us to bring you more focused information, giving you more of what you need to know, and less of what you don't.

Packt is a modern, yet unique publishing company, which focuses on producing quality, cutting-edge books for communities of developers, administrators, and newbies alike. For more information, please visit our website: www.packtpub.com.

Writing for Packt

We welcome all inquiries from people who are interested in authoring. Book proposals should be sent to author@packtpub.com. If your book idea is still at an early stage and you would like to discuss it first before writing a formal book proposal, contact us; one of our commissioning editors will get in touch with you.

We're not just looking for published authors; if you have strong technical skills but no writing experience, our experienced editors can help you develop a writing career, or simply get some additional reward for your expertise.

**Microsoft Silverlight 5 Data
and Services Cookbook**

Gill Cleeren   Kevin Dockx   [PACKT] enterprise

Microsoft Silverlight 5 Data and Services Cookbook

ISBN: 978-1-849683-50-0   Paperback: 662 pages

Over 100 practical recipes for creating rich,
data-driven, business applications in Silverlight 5

1. Design and develop rich data-driven business
    applications in Silverlight and Windows Phone
    7 following best practices using this book and
    eBook

2. Rapidly interact with services and handle
    multiple sources of data within Silverlight and
    Windows Phone 7 business applications

**Responsive Web Design
with HTML5 and CSS3**

Learn responsive design using HTML5 and CSS3 to adapt
websites to any browser or screen size

Ben Frain   PACKT

Responsive Web Design with HTML5 and CSS3

ISBN: 978-1-849693-18-9   Paperback: 324 pages

Learn responsive design using HTML5 and CSS3 to
adapt websites to any browser or screen size

1. Everything needed to code websites in HTML5
    and CSS3 that are responsive to every device or
    screen size

2. Learn the main new features of HTML5 and
    use CSS3's stunning new capabilities including
    animations, transitions and transformations

3. Real world examples show how to
    progressively enhance a responsive design
    while providing fall backs for older browsers

Please check **www.PacktPub.com** for information on our titles

HTML5 Canvas Cookbook

ISBN: 978-1-849691-36-9   Paperback: 348 pages

Over 80 recipes to revolutionize the web experience with HTML5 Canvas

1. The quickest way to get up to speed with HTML5 Canvas application and game development

2. Create stunning 3D visualizations and games without Flash

3. Written in a modern, unobtrusive, and objected oriented JavaScript style so that the code can be reused in your own applications.

HTML5 Games Development by Example: Beginner's Guide

ISBN: 978-1-849691-26-0   Paperback: 352 pages

Create six fun games using the latest HTML5, Canvas, CSS, and JavaScript techniques

1. Learn HTML5 game development by building six fun example projects

2. Full, clear explanations of all the essential techniques

3. Covers puzzle games, action games, multiplayer, and Box 2D physics

4. Use the Canvas with multiple layers and sprite sheets for rich graphical games

Please check **www.PacktPub.com** for information on our titles

www.ingramcontent.com/pod-product-compliance
Lightning Source LLC
Chambersburg PA
CBHW060200060326
40690CB00018B/4181